PRISON RACE

PRISON RACE

Renford Reese

Carolina Academic Press

Durham, North Carolina

Library of Congress Cataloging-in-Publication Data

Reese, Renford, 1967 -
    Prison race / by Renford Reese.
        p. cm.
    ISBN 1-59460-183-6
    1. Discrimination in criminal justice administration--United States. 2.
African American prisoners. 3. Crime and race--United States. 4.
Racism--United States. 5. African American prisoners--California. 6.
Corrections--California. I. Title.

    HV9950.R434 2006
    365'.608996073--dc22

                                                    2005027384

CAROLINA ACADEMIC PRESS

700 Kent Street
Durham, North Carolina 27701
Telephone (919) 489-7486
Fax (919) 493-5668
www.cap-press.com

Printed in the United States of America
Cover photo by Alan Wade

- ◆ To those who are entangled in the system and unaware of the **big picture.**

- ◆ To lawmakers who have the courage to do the right thing.

Contents

PRISON RACE

Introduction

This book has been written primarily for those members of the public—including lawmakers—who might be unaware of the damage wrought on U.S. society by decades of counterproductive criminal justice policies. In these pages, two fundamental questions are addressed: *Why have lawmakers embraced counterproductive criminal justice policies? What have been the consequences of these policies?*

> The subject of prisons and corrections may tempt some of you to tune out. You may think, well, I am not a criminal lawyer. The prison system is not my problem. I might tune in again when he gets to a different subject. In my submission you have the duty to stay tuned in. The subject is the concern and responsibility of every member of our profession and every citizen. This is your justice system; these are your prisons. (Supreme Court Justice Anthony Kennedy, addressing the American Bar Association annual meeting, 2003)

During the past two decades in the United States, there has been a race to incarcerate. And one race in particular has been impacted by discriminatory and unjust corrections policies driven by the promises of politicians to "get tough on crime." Although this book is more about criminal justice policies than it is about race, it examines these policies in the context of their impact on the African American male population.

Prison Race is a double entendre.

The federal government's extraordinarily slow response to the desperate black victims of Hurricane Katrina in New Orleans and the surrounding areas has forced the U.S. to examine, once again, its most recalcitrant sociocultural phenomenon: racial bias.

3

The United States has the world's largest per capita prison population. The incarcerated population in this country has topped two million. The repeat offender rate is more than 50 percent. Some 47 million Americans have federal or state criminal records. A disproportionate number of these are African American. Blacks make up 12.6 percent of the total population but 49 percent of those incarcerated. One of every four black men between the ages of 16 and 26 is in prison, in jail, on parole, or on probation. Young black men are six times more likely than white youths to be incarcerated by adult courts for comparable crimes.

Race, in the U.S. criminal justice system, significantly affects the probability that a person will be convicted of a crime. It also tends to determine the severity of the sentence. U.S. criminal justice policies have had the most adverse effect on black men. While I focus in *Prison Race* on this population, it is important to remember that Latino men and African American women are also disproportionately represented in U.S. prisons.

I chose to feature California's corrections policies in this book because its corrections department is the largest in the nation. In addition, California's policies—including the "three strikes" law—are often emulated by other states. For comparative purposes, I examined the corrections policies of several states. Each of them differs in significant ways. However, many have in common a reluctance to embrace progressive or humanistic corrections policies. Few states have found substantive ways to curb alarmingly high recidivism rates.

My first book, *American Paradox: Young Black Men*, examined one model of black masculinity embraced by many young black men. The **gangsta-thug** tough-guy model has manifested itself in a wide range of counterproductive behaviors, from underachievement in school to violent, criminal acts. After *American Paradox* was published in 2004, I realized I wanted to do outreach to the most troubled and vulnerable black men: those who were incarcerated. I pledged to make monthly visits to California state prisons to motivate these men and enlighten them about navigating through an unjust system.

Because the California Institute for Men in Chino is the prison facility closest to my university, I visit it most frequently. I speak to groups of twenty inmates, with an average age of 25, about living a purpose-driven life and what it will take for successful reentry into society. After my lectures to the inmates, however, I experience dissonance. On one hand, I am attempting to motivate these individuals to be better people and more productive citizens. On the other, the government has devised a complex web of restrictive policies that make it almost impossible for them to succeed. No matter how inspirational my words, the corrections policies of the state will undermine them.

When inmates are released from confinement, nobody trusts them. They cannot get jobs or housing. In many cases they are denied a driver's license and public assistance. If they make a single bad decision, no matter how minor, they can be sent back to prison for violating their parole agreement. These are some of the reasons why the majority of those who have completed their sentences return to prison within six months of their release.

No one benefits from astronomically high recidivism rates. In the long term, no one benefits from punish-only corrections strategies. Public safety is an ideologically neutral priority for all lawmakers. However, public safety is undermined, not enhanced, when policies and laws construct obstacles that prevent ex-offenders from successfully reintegrating into society. During the 1980s and 1990s, the "get tough on crime" mantra became the central theme of both liberal and conservative politicians. Though politically expedient, the "punish, punish, punish" philosophy for confronting criminal activity has proved to be shortsighted and counterproductive. States are only now beginning to see the irrationality of two decades of callous, hyper-punitive policies.

It is counterintuitive to spend billions of dollars on punishment and incarceration but only a fraction of that amount on preventive measures, such as K–12 education; preschool, after-school, and recreational programs; and job training. Barack Obama's inspiring speech at the 2004 Democratic National Convention resonated with millions of Americans. He issued an intriguing appeal to the U.S. government when he stated, "No, people don't expect government to solve all their problems. But they sense, deep in their bones, that with just a change in priorities, we can make sure that every child in America has a decent shot at life, and that the doors of opportunity remain open to all. They know we can do better. And they want that choice."

Prison Race presents a reasoned argument in favor of changing priorities where criminal justice policies are concerned.

Methodology

For this book, I surveyed, with the help of student assistants, 500 residents of Southern California to get their opinions about various corrections policies. I also interviewed and/or surveyed 35 individuals who are closely connected with corrections systems, including inmates in California prisons and parolees in the Georgia corrections system. My questions to prisoners and parolees ranged from inquiries about their prison experiences to their plans once they were released. One insightful inmate provided a particularly riveting account of prison life and culture.

I conducted interviews with corrections officers, parole officers, prison educational representatives, prison caseworkers, police officers, and several free felons. I also used reports from nonprofit organizations and academic institutions to buttress my analysis. I integrated data from the U.S. Justice Department's Bureau of Justice Statistics, an indispensable resource in research on criminal justice policies. My research was also enhanced by the use of journal articles, books, and newspapers. Along with the aforementioned sources of data, I relied on my prison visits and my interactions with hundreds of inmates during a sixteen-month period to assist me in my analyses for this book.

Overview

Chapter One examines the issue of discriminatory criminal justice policies in the U.S. in the broader context of Constitutional principles, social justice, and liberal democracy. The scales of justice symbolize, among other things, proportionality between crime and punishment. Today's criminal justice system betrays its own philosophical foundation, the ideal that it is better to let nine guilty people go free than to convict one innocent person. Current policies counter centuries of reasoned thought on the subject of crime and punishment, including the Enlightenment philosophy that informed the framers of the U.S. Constitution.

Chapter Two reviews the recalcitrant issue of race, including the struggle for civil rights in the U.S. and the national legacy of discriminatory criminal justice policies. An array of methods has been used to demonize African Americans and solidify whites' fear of "dangerous" and "savage" blacks. Whether through lynching, capital punishment, or police brutality, U.S. society has failed to live up to the egalitarian spirit of the Constitution and has exacted an incalculable toll on the esteem of black men.

Chapter Three presents the story of Michael "Quake" Fisher, in his own words. Quake was convicted of manslaughter in 1993 and sentenced to twelve years in prison at the age of 19. In 2004, he wrote me a letter from Centinela State Prison in Imperial, California, to tell me he agreed with the thesis of my first book, *American Paradox*. I subsequently visited him in prison and asked him to write an essay about prison culture. Quake discusses all aspects of prison life in a way no scholar could. His insights are riveting.

Chapter Four identifies the obstacles inmates face as they try to reenter society. Ex-convicts are stigmatized and routinely refused jobs, housing, and public assistance. There is a great deal of emphasis in political discourse about public safety, and yet lawmakers fail to acknowledge the correlation between public safety and recidivism.

Chapter Five explores the impact of various ignoble laws implemented by the criminal justice system during the past two decades, including "three strikes" laws, mandatory minimum sentencing laws, and laws that try teens as adults. This chapter deconstructs how lawmakers have adopted simple and short-term solutions to deal with very complex and long-term problems.

Chapter Six examines prison conditions in the U.S. Although the public was shocked and outraged at the callous and insensitive treatment of Iraqi prisoners at Abu Ghraib, those familiar with conditions in U.S. prisons were not surprised. Multiple human rights violations exist within the walls of our prisons. They are woefully overcrowded. Inmates are given substandard health care, sexually assaulted, warehoused and punished without opportunities for rehabilitation. The current state of prison conditions in this country is an embarrassment to a government that touts itself around the world as the model of democracy, fairness, and justice.

Chapter Seven explores corporate crime and the preferential treatment of white-collar criminals in the U.S. The tradition of retributive justice uses an offender's damage to the state as a criterion for sentencing. Some 60 percent of inmates in prison are incarcerated for nonviolent crimes with an insignificant impact on the state. While nonviolent street criminals spend time in maximum-security prisons for drug possession or check fraud that sometimes amounts to a few hundred dollars, corporate criminals who have bilked hundreds of millions of dollars from shareholders and taxpayers are sentenced to minimum-security prisons commonly referred to as "Club Feds" because of their comfortable accommodations. This type of disproportionate treatment is glaringly unjust.

Chapter Eight examines the "business" of prisons, including the positioning of prison guard unions as influential interest groups, the proliferation of prisons, and the role of prison labor in a cycle of capitalistic exploitation. Regions that lost manufacturing jobs in the 1970s and 1980s and were left out of the economic boom of the 1990s have come to rely on prisons as primary sources of employment. Big companies involved in the prison industry enjoy billions of dollars in income. Many states spend more of their budgets building and maintaining prisons than they do building and maintaining universities. Businesses take advantage of cheap prison labor, which shrinks the number of jobs in society. The irony is that prisoners have a better chance of working at a job in prison than they do finding one outside of prison.

The final components of *Prison Race* are appendices A, B, and C.

Appendix A presents the results of the survey of 500 residents of Southern California regarding their opinions about corrections policies. Survey data are classified according to race of respondent; e.g., African American, White, Latino, Asian, and Other.

Appendix B provides a blueprint for the establishment of a Reintegration Academy at Cal Poly Pomona University. This is proposed as a model program to give young ex-offenders the tools and the skills they need to reenter society successfully. Parolees from the California Youth Authority, ages 18 to 25, would participate in a ten-week program focusing on academic, professional, and personal development training. Those who complete the program will continue on to community colleges, vocational training programs, universities, and jobs.

Appendix C contains poetry and rap lyrics composed by prison inmates. Writing is a therapeutic exercise for many, and more than a few are gifted writers. They have a unique way of fusing harsh realities with dreams in their work, with palpable excitement and enthusiasm. When I lectured to inmates I told them I was holding a writing contest, and the ten best entries would be published in this book. The only requirement was that the writing be about the inmate's experience with the prison system. Inmates responded with words that give insight into the reality of the prison experience and are true to the inmate's raw emotions.

Chapter 1

Social Injustice

On August 9, 2003, U.S. Supreme Court Justice Anthony Kennedy delivered an intriguing speech at the annual meeting of the American Bar Association. It can be summarized as an indictment of U.S. prisons and the corrections system. Kennedy, a Reagan appointee, highlighted the problems of racial inequality in the system and urged those in the legal professions to embrace the law with compassion and humanism.

> We have a greater responsibility. As a profession, and as a people, we should know what happens after the prisoner is taken away. To be sure, the prisoner has violated the social contract; to be sure he must be punished to vindicate the law, to acknowledge the suffering of the victim, and to deter future crimes. Still, the prisoner is a person; still, he or she is part of the family of humankind. (Kennedy 2003)

The U.S. criminal justice system has consistently contradicted the principles of American democracy. The victimization and unequal treatment of minorities in the courts, police departments, and corrections facilities are inconsistent with the U.S. Constitution. More specifically, this treatment undermines the significance of the equal protection clause of the Fourteenth Amendment. Race-motivated arrests, sentencing, and incarcerations highlight the injustices of this system. As Justice Kennedy states, "Embedded in democracy is the idea of progress. Democracy addresses injustice and corrects it. The progress is not automatic. It requires a sustained exercise of political will; and political will is shaped by rational public discourse" (Kennedy 2003).

The U.S. was founded on noble and egalitarian principles in service of the public good. Framers of the U.S. Constitution embraced the writings of John Locke, who argued that people have natural rights that cannot be taken away. The basic natural rights are life, liberty, and property. However, on some points the framers diverged from the Lockean tradition, which was based on the idea of politics of majority interest. In the Federalist Papers, James Madison, Alexander Hamilton, and John Jay outlined a system of governance in which the U.S. would balance the interests of the majority while protecting the rights of the minority. In Federalist 51, Madison asks, on what basis can any majority ever be found? Not on the basis of self-interest hostile to the public good, he argues. Perhaps it is self-interest hostile to the public good that has led to the disparities in the current U.S. criminal justice system.

It is paramount in a democracy that the rule of law is obeyed, and this requires keeping the peace. Hence, the American democracy is an experiment in law enforcement and peacekeeping in which police are called upon to provide security and protect liberty in order to uphold the ultimate purpose of government. James Madison stated, "Justice is the end of government ... it has ever been and ever will be pursued until it be obtained, or until liberty be lost in the pursuit." Indeed, it was Madison's Federalist 10 that presaged the nation's struggles to preserve both liberty and order (Delattre 1996).

Some suggest the role of police in U.S. society is crime prevention. In fact, the police have multiple roles in the U.S. criminal justice system: peacekeeping, maintenance of order, and social service delivery (Delattre 1996). The police are just one dimension of a multilayered criminal justice system that involves the courts, judges, lawyers, parole officers, and corrections officials. In the past decade, however, politicians and the American public, through voter-approved laws, have had the greatest impact on the criminal justice system. These two entities have constructed a criminal justice system that is seen in the eyes of many minorities as unfair and unjust. This system lacks legitimacy with a significant sector of the U.S. population.

Since the Rodney King beating in 1991, the situation for young black men has become drastically worse. Civil liberties law in the U.S. has evolved significantly in the past forty years. However, during the last decade these laws have increasingly been applied unequally. What does this say about the U.S. model of liberal democracy? Statistical disparities and unequal treatment between blacks and whites suggest the U.S. criminal justice system is violating its own Constitutional principles.

This chapter attempts to highlight, from a philosophical perspective, the contradictions between America's noble creed and ignoble deeds.

Freedom and Justice

Some philosophers look at the concept of social justice in the context of freedom. For instance, Orlando Patterson, who is a sociologist as well as a philosopher, discusses the notion of civic freedom, which he defines as the capacity of adult members of a community to participate in its life and governance (1991). Eric Foner discusses the notion of freedom in the context of rights. Natural rights are those that are inherent to one's humanity, such as life, liberty, and the pursuit of happiness. Civil rights are based on equal treatment under the law, which is paramount for the defense of natural rights. Martin Luther King Jr.'s four conceptions of freedom were born out of the civil rights movement. King's definition of liberal freedom is the absence of arbitrary legal or institutional restrictions on individuals coupled with equal protection under the law. Freedom as autonomy is based on an individual's ability to internalize a state of autonomy, self-determination, and respect. Participatory freedom is the right of an individual to participate fully in civic life. Collective deliverance revolves around a group's liberation from external control; e.g., slavery, captivity, or oppression (Walton and Smith 2000).

The concept of the **social contract** is at the foundation of today's liberal democracies. This is a conceptual reference to the relationship that should exist between a government and its citizens. The general principle of the social contract assumes that citizens must subject themselves to the authority of the government and government should protect the natural rights of citizens (Barker 1966). Enlightenment thinkers Thomas Hobbes, Jean-Jacques Rousseau, John Locke, and Cesare Beccaria have discussed the social contract in their writings. Hobbes and Locke disagreed on the role of the government in the contract. For Hobbes, the government represented the **leviathan**, an all-powerful entity to which citizens completely submit and surrender their rights. Locke, however, wrote that people never completely give up their rights. According to Locke, government was legitimate as long as it reflected the will of the people and preserved the natural rights of its citizens. If the government reneged on this contractual position, it should be replaced (Knepper 2003).

Framers of the U.S. Constitution agreed with Locke ([1690] 1967) that people have natural rights to life, liberty, and property. These cannot be taken away. However, their support for the institution of slavery showed that the framers agreed with Lockean principles only in the abstract.

In theory, the U.S. criminal justice system is based on principles of fairness and equity outlined in the Constitution. The Preamble states that the purpose of our government is to "establish justice, insure domestic tranquility, provide for the common defense, promote the general welfare, and secure the blessings of liberty to ourselves and our posterity" (Kelman 1996, A-4). The Bill of Rights, a fundamental component of the Constitution, protects civil liberties. In addition, the Fourteenth Amendment provides equal protection under the law. Ostensibly, the staunch protection of civil liberties and equal protection of citizens is what separates the U.S. from totalitarian governments. Under totalitarian regimes, police, acting as agents of the government, have no regard for the basic civil liberties of individuals. In these regimes, individuals do not have equal protection under the law.

Social Justice Theory

Philosophers through the centuries have attempted to define the concept of social justice. Its definition remains both amorphous and contextual. Plato and Aristotle constructed definitions that are not applicable to the discussion of racial bias and unfairness in the U.S. criminal justice system. In his *Republic*, Plato speaks of a just state consisting of three social classes: workers, soldiers, and rulers. Performance of the job of each class without interference from other classes is regarded as just. In *Ethics*, Aristotle states that all men seek edaimonia, a state of happiness. The pursuit of happiness compels all men to optimize their potential. These great thinkers laid the foundations of philosophical discourse on social justice (Reese 2004, 147).

According to Immanuel Kant's concept of ethical formalism, if a behavior cannot be categorized as "just and proper," it is immoral. John Stuart Mill's theory of justice builds on the utilitarian philosophy of Jeremy Bentham. Utilitarianism holds that justice revolves around the "greatest good for the greatest possible number of people." In many instances, the U.S. has adopted a utilitarian philosophy when determining public policies. On the surface, this principle is just and equitable. However, under scrutiny, the concept of utilitarianism is flawed, especially in the context of minority rights. A true democracy cannot flourish unless the interests of the majority are balanced with the interests of the minority. Espousing the "greatest good for the greatest number" philosophy makes a society vulnerable to what Alexis de Tocqueville refers to as the "tyranny of the majority." If there is a community in which 90 percent of the population is of one ethnicity, for example, and the remaining 10 percent is of another, what happens when the majority decides they do not like the minority and collectively determines they should lock all members of the minority group in jail? There is no legitimate provocation for the incarceration of the minority group, but the majority decides they would be better off without the minority group's presence in the community. This policy decision is utilitarian—the greatest number of people have decided what is in their own best self-interest—but it is clearly flawed and detrimental to one group of citizens. In a democracy, it is incumbent upon the government to protect the rights of all, including the rights of the minority.

Contemporary social philosopher Howard Zinn helps us to understand the concept of social justice. In *Disobedience and Democracy*, Zinn states there is no moral imperative to obey an immoral law, unless the very idea of obeying a law has legitimacy and moral value. In other words, there is nothing inherently immoral about disobeying a law that is unjust. John Rawls's theory of justice revolves around the themes of equal liberty and democratic equality. His **veil of ignorance** and **original position** concepts provide a normative framework for ethical and just decisionmaking. Rawls's conceptual framework is relevant to the U.S. criminal justice system. According to Rawls, no one is aware of their lot in life: their social or economic status, their personal or professional identity. The original position can be taken as a theoretical starting point for decisionmakers. Just and equitable decisions would be the outcome of proceeding from the original position to making decisions behind the veil of ignorance. For example, let us return to the community made up of 90 percent of one ethnicity and 10 percent of another. We put all these individuals in the original position behind a veil of ignorance. There is still an initiative circulating in the community to jail every member of the minority group. However, using Rawls's concept that everyone is unaware of their status, no one is certain if they are in the minority population. Therefore, no one is certain whether they will be victims of the "jail the minority" policy. In this scenario, the people reject the policy and do what is just. The brilliance of Rawls's theory of justice is that it does not rely on altruism or the good-heartedness of people to make just decisions. Instead, people are compelled by their own self-interest to make just decisions. This conceptual framework involves empathy and theoretical role-playing. Would politicians enthusiastically vote for unfair, unjust, and punitive criminal justice policies if they were unaware of both their lot in life and their status? Would they vote for such policies if there were potential that they or their family members could be adversely affected? (Rawls 1971).

While many theorists and philosophers have discussed the issue of justice in the abstract, Martin Luther King Jr.'s conception of social justice is the most relevant to the plight of African Americans in today's society. Indeed, we should use King's definition of social justice as the context for deciding the justness of the U.S. criminal justice system. King discusses social justice in a dialectical framework that exposes the glaring contradictions between the nation's noble creed and its ignoble deeds. During the most tumultuous period of the U.S. civil rights movement, King was arrested in the city of Birmingham, Alabama, for protesting the unjust laws of segregation in the South. While in jail, on April 16, 1963, King poignantly highlighted the contradictions in America's system of justice in his famous "Letter From Birmingham Jail."

Injustice anywhere is a threat to justice everywhere.... Perhaps it is easy for those who have never felt the stinging darts of segregation to say, "Wait." But when you have seen vicious mobs lynch your mothers and fathers at will and drown your sisters and brothers at whim; when you have seen hate-filled policemen curse, kick and even kill your Black brothers and sisters; when you see the vast majority of your twenty million Negro brothers smothering in an airtight cage of poverty in the midst of an affluent society ... then you will understand why we find it difficult to wait. (King 1964, 65–69)

What are the criteria that render a law unjust? King lists four: (1) if it degrades human personality; (2) if it binds one group and not another; (3) if it is enacted by an authority not truly representative; and (4) if, though just in itself, it is unjustly applied. The presence of one of these factors is sufficient to render a law unjust (Crawford 1973). The U.S. has created a system of criminal justice that meets all four of King's criteria for unjust laws. In fact, the U.S. system does not consistently conform to any of the several accepted theories of social justice. What sets the U.S. system apart from the theories of Kant, Mill, Rawls, Hobbes, Locke, and Zinn is the fact that its laws are unjustly applied. Not only is the U.S. system incongruent with the various theories of justice, this system is unequal to other systems of criminal justice in the Western world (Reese 2004, 149).

Critical Race Theory

Critical race theory in the U.S. developed from critical legal studies, which were developed to analyze and deconstruct legal doctrines. Lawyers, legal scholars, and civil rights activists interested in the relationship of race, racism, and power started the critical race theory movement in the mid-1970s. Derrick Bell, professor of law at New York University, is considered the father of this movement (Delgado and Stefancic 2001). The primary outcome of critical legal studies is that law cannot be relied upon to protect those who are without power. According to this school of thought, law is not designed to construct justice but instead is designed to protect those who already hold power. As a derivative of critical legal studies, critical race theory posits that the justice system is manipulated to legitimize white supremacy and maintain a rule of law (Russell 1999).

The two overarching themes that guided the framers of the U.S. Constitution were protecting private property and limiting the power of the government to avoid tyranny (Walton and Smith 2000). The serious concern of protecting the minority who owned property laid the foundation for an elitist democracy. In the context of critical race theory, the criminal justice system has upheld the principle of protecting the privileged.

The criminal justice system in the U.S. represents the interests of the power structure; it plays a **power maintenance** role in society. As Richard Ropers and Dan Pence state, "The history, preoccupation, and structured role of the criminal justice system for adults and juveniles has ensured the political, social, and economic subordination of this nation's racial minorities" (Ropers and Pence 1995, 187). James Baldwin captures the essence of the problem in his 1964 essay, "Fifth Avenue, Uptown: A Letter From Harlem."

> The only way to police the ghetto is to be oppressive. None of the police commissioner's men, even with the best will in the world, have any way of understanding the lives led by the people they swagger in twos and threes controlling. Their very presence is an insult, and it would be, even if they spent their entire day feeding gumdrops to children. They represent the force of the White world, and that [force's] intentions are simply ... to keep the Black man corralled up here, in his place. The badge, the gun in the holster, and the swinging club make vivid what will happen should his rebellion become overt. (Baldwin 1964, 60–65)

The U.S. has based its moral sensibilities on a unique individualism identified and described by Alexis de Tocqueville in 1835. Michael Lewis observes that individualism is at the core of America's culture of inequality. The assumption is that with hard work everyone can achieve personal success. This bold notion does not take into account the oppressive social structure that exists in the U.S. (Lewis 1993). The idea that anyone can be successful in America is quixotic. It does not mirror the reality that social conditions have restricted many young black males from attaining equal opportunities.

Race and the Criminal Justice System

As the science of gathering DNA has evolved in the past decade, so has the evidence of foul play. Hundreds of innocent people have been wrongfully incarcerated. DNA evidence has exposed the U.S. criminal justice system as being terribly discriminatory and flawed. A 2004 study of 328 criminal cases over the past fifteen years in which the convicted person was eventually exonerated due to DNA evidence suggests that there are thousands of innocent people incarcerated today. Some 29 percent of those in prison for rape are black; blacks also account for 65 percent of those ultimately exonerated for this crime. Rapes of white women by black men represent less than 10 percent of all rapes. Nevertheless, in half of the rape exonerations black men had been falsely accused of raping white women. These startling statistics suggest that the American justice system is unfair. In spirit and in practice, the criminal justice system has failed to embrace the egalitarian principles found in the Constitution (Liptak 2004, A14).

In U.S. society, the police have acted as agents of the system. Indeed, the white-dominated social structure has been legitimized in police behavior. Those without power have come to see the police as the enemy. The themes of racial profiling and police brutality have resonated throughout U.S. history. What the Kerner report found to be true in 1968 remains true today: "... To many Negroes police have come to symbolize white power, white racism, and white repression" (Kerner Commission 1968, 206).

On March 3, 1991, the infamous Rodney King beating occurred and was captured on videotape. Since that date, there have been alarmingly frequent cases of police brutality, among them the tragic incidents involving Amadou Diallo, Abner Louima, Demetrius DuBose, Irvin Landrum, Thomas Jones, Timothy Thomas, and Donovan Jackson (Reese 2004). Each of these cases is a clear example of police officers using unjustified and excessive force to subdue black men. They represent only the high-profile instances of race-driven police brutality. There are many others. Some remain unreported; others are given scant attention by the press. Racial profiling, excessive force, and police brutality reflect a blatant disregard for civil liberties and have magnified the flaws in U.S. liberal democracy.

According to self-reported data compiled by the U.S. Public Health Service in 1999, African Americans constitute about 14 percent of the nation's users of illegal drugs. Yet they make up 35 percent of those arrested for drug possession, 55 percent of those convicted for drug possession, and 74 percent of those sentenced to serve time for their crimes (Cole 2000). According to Human Rights Watch (2002), relative to population, black men are admitted to state and federal prisons on drug charges at 13.4 times the rate of white men. In seven states, blacks make up between 80 and 90 percent of all drug offenders sent to prison. Black men are incarcerated for all offenses at 8.2 times the rate of whites. One in every 20 black men is in state or federal prison, compared to one in 180 white men.

The U.S. is incarcerating an entire generation of minority men. This trend has a significant impact on minority communities. Those who are incarcerated do not have jobs, pay taxes, or care for their children. Many cannot vote. Because 45 states have voting restrictions for offenders, at least one in seven black men has lost the right to vote, if only temporarily. Parolees are denied their right to vote in 32 states. This felony disenfranchisement restricts approximately four million Americans—most of them minorities—from voting. Some 31 percent of the black men in Florida and Alabama are prohibited from voting because of felony convictions. On the national level, 13 percent of black men are disenfranchised because of felony convictions compared to 2 percent of white men (Reese 2004, 156).

In 2005, the U.S. Supreme Court declined to hear a case that challenged Florida's lifetime voting ban for anyone convicted of a felony. In Florida, not only can felons not vote, they cannot serve on juries or hold a state-issued occupational license (New Journal 2005, 04A).

Racial bias in the U.S. criminal justice system can be blamed indirectly on a number of factors, including biased police, juries, judges, and politicians. All of these groups have been criticized for their decisions and behavior. But prosecutors have consistently been given a free pass about exercising sometimes subtle and sometimes blatant racial bias. They wield unchecked power in ways that are virtually invisible to those outside the system. Slipping under the radar of protests about mean-spirited politicians and overly aggressive police, prosecutors go about their jobs unfettered by scrutiny, often sabotaging the lives of thousands of minorities and their families. In his stinging essay, "Absolute Power, Absolute Corruption," Robert Owen examines the destructive discretionary power of prosecutors:

> ... what we encounter much more frequently in the contemporary American criminal justice system is better described as *overreaching*: oppressive tactics born of systemic institutional arrangements that reward (or fail to punish) prosecutors who "cut corners" in pursuit of a conviction. The government's resources and power so dramatically outweigh those of the accused that prosecutors, rather than scrutinizing their own behavior to guard against abuses of power, habitually focus only on their won-lost record and its political consequences. (Owen 2003, 23)

Owen identifies a number of ways in which overreaching leads prosecutors to abuse of power, including overreaching by concealing evidence that might help the accused and overreaching by overcharging and thus coercing "cooperation." He also highlights the failure of the mass media to spotlight either prosecutorial overreaching or the legal system's continuing refusal to punish prosecutors for oppressive and unfair conduct (Owen 2003, 24–27).

Prosecutorial abuse of power is a flaw in the institutional fabric of the criminal justice system. How can a liberal democracy that prides itself on the separation of power, and the meticulous monitoring of abuse of power, allow prosecutors to wield absolute power?

The Sixth Amendment to the U.S. Constitution states that one who is accused of a crime is entitled to "the assistance of Counsel for his defense." In 1963, in the case of *Gideon v. Wainright*, the Supreme Court applied the Sixth Amendment, ruling that a poor person is constitutionally guaranteed legal representation. A person without means who faces felony charges "cannot be assured a fair trial unless counsel is provided for him." However:

Many of the men, women, and children sent to prison in the United States every day are processed through courts without the legal representation that is indispensable to a fair trial, a reliable verdict, and a just sentence. Eighty percent of people accused of crimes are unable to afford a lawyer to defend them. (Bright 2003, 6)

While some public defenders are dedicated to representing the accused poor with vigor, others do not expend sufficient energy or effort to mount a credible defense. Inadequate legal counsel is often the equivalent of no legal counsel. Lackluster representation of the poor does not embrace the spirit of the Sixth Amendment. As Stephen Bright candidly states, "While public defender offices or dedicated lawyers capably defend some of the accused, far more are assigned lawyers who work under crushing caseloads, are paid so little that they devote little time to the cases, and lack the time, knowledge, resources, and often even the inclination to defend a case properly" (Bright 2003, 7).

Scales of Justice

In 1994 Congress passed the Violent Crime Control and Law Enforcement Act. As a result of this legislation, many states implemented "three strikes and you're out" laws. These state that if a person is convicted of three crimes, the sentence for the third crime will be 25 years in prison to life in prison. This law was intended to apply to those who committed three violent crimes. However, it has been grossly misused. In March 2003 the U. S. Supreme Court, in a 5-4 decision, upheld the legitimacy of three strikes laws. The Court ruled in two cases that California's three strikes law did not yield "grossly disproportionate" sentences in violation of the Eighth Amendment. In the case of *Lockyer v. Andrade*, the Supreme Court upheld the indeterminate life sentence with no possibility of parole for 50 years that Leandro Andrade received for stealing $153 worth of children's videotapes from K-mart. In *Ewing v. California*, Ewing was sentenced to 25 years to life for grand theft after he stole three golf clubs worth a total of $1,200. This offense also qualified as a third strike (Chemerinsky 2003).

Now lawmakers and the public seem to be realizing that the hard-edged philosophy of simply locking inmates up and throwing away the key is not working. The "punish, punish, punish" approach that has been embraced during the past two decades has proven to be ineffective and counterproductive. Indeed, the situation in California makes for an interesting case study. California law states the purpose of incarceration is punishment, not rehabilitation. Its correctional system is the largest in the U.S. The state that embraced tough sentencing laws in the 1980s and 1990s has experienced the highest rate of recidivism in the nation. Over 80 percent of inmates released from California prisons in 2002 returned within six months. Although California's crime rate has plummeted during the past two decades, its prison population has soared, from 20,000 to 163,000. The amount the state must budget to run its prisons has increased to more than $6 billion (Wood 2004, 2).

Historically, religion has played a significant role in the rehabilitation of inmates. In their confinement and solitude many inmates "see the light." Prison ministries have done exemplary jobs of prison outreach and embracing the egalitarian spirit of the U.S. Constitution. In many instances, prison ministry sessions are the only encounters that inmates have with the concepts of love, compassion, charity, and forgiveness. Ministries that are true to the words of their faith are not afraid to reach out to ex-prisoners and attempt to help them successfully reenter society. Churches have proven to be the most sympathetic institutions in reaching out to what Karl Marx called the **lumpen proletariat**-those individuals on the fringes of society. The faith-based approach to rehabilitating prisoners and ex-prisoners is important. However, the government has primary responsibility to provide for the needs of the truly disadvantaged in our society. Whether it is the physically or mentally disabled, the destitute, or the elderly, the government has stepped in to provide assistance. This compassionate philosophy should not be set aside when it comes to prison inmates and ex-offenders. They too are truly disadvantaged.

The classicists adamantly believed that the relationship between crime and punishment should be proportional. This balance is one of the symbolized meanings of the scales of justice. Italian Enlightenment thinker Cesare Beccaria laid the foundation for classical thought on crime and punishment in his seminal work *Dei delitti e delle pene* (*Of Crimes and Punishments*), first published in 1764. According to Beccaria, the government could encourage lawful behavior by carefully measuring the proportionality of crimes and punishment. "It is better to prevent crimes than to punish them," he argues. "That is the ultimate end of every good legislation." The utilitarian philosopher Jeremy Bentham states, "Punishment, which, if it goes beyond the limit of necessity, is a pure evil" (Knepper 2003, 36–38). Politicians and policymakers who have constructed the policies that constitute our current criminal justice system, in which crime and punishment are no longer proportional, are countering centuries of rational thought.

Alexis de Tocqueville stated in 1835 in *Democracy in America* that the unequal treatment of blacks in America would lead to a revolution. He predicted the Civil War. Unequal treatment has historically been the impetus for most of the race riots in the U.S., including those in 1919, 1965, 1992, and the most recent, in Cincinnati.

Racial polarization, racial bias, and racial insensitivity have threatened to undermine the strong foundation of a number of American institutions in addition to the criminal justice system. The passage of the Thirteenth, Fourteenth, and Fifteenth Amendments to the Constitution ended the federal government's official endorsement of racial discrimination. However, blatant discrimination still exists. Racial profiling, excessive force, police brutality, racial disparities in the system, and blatant disregard for civil liberties have magnified the flaws in our democratic society. The U.S. criminal justice system meets all four of King's criteria for unjust laws; and it is inconsistent with the precepts of social justice because its laws are unjustly applied. In our system the fate of one American is inextricably intertwined with the fate of another. It is a disservice to all if we turn our back on the ideal embodied in our founding philosophy, that it is better to let nine guilty people go free than to convict one innocent person.

As the great African American leader Booker T. Washington stated in his 1895 Atlanta Compromise Address, "The laws of changeless justice bind oppressor with oppressed; and close as sin and suffering joined. We march to fate abreast" (Washington [1901] 1995). King added, eloquently, as he wrote from the Birmingham jail: "We are caught in an inescapable network of mutuality, tied in a single garment of destiny" (King 1964, 65).

U.S. society made its first attempt to live up to noble egalitarian principles during Radical Reconstruction (1866–1877). Since this period, incremental progress has been coupled with staggering setbacks for blacks in America. This disturbing pattern of dealing with the "Negro Problem" has been, and remains, an American dilemma. The U.S. cannot continue to ignore the unequal treatment of a significant sector of its population by its criminal justice system. The health and well-being of America's liberal democracy are undermined by this unjust system. The U.S. cannot tout its model of democracy to the world until it remedies the systemic race-based problems that lay at its foundation. In a postmodern era, the United States cannot afford to revert to the unjust laws of an earlier time, one marked by barbarism. The cornerstone of a civil society is respect for the heterogeneous. The role of government and all of its agents is to carry out duties in ways that exemplify fairness, justice, and equity. The legitimacy of the U.S. model of democracy depends on its embrace of these fundamental principles.

References

Baldwin, James. 1964. *Nobody Knows My Name: More Notes from a Native Son*. London: Penguin.

Barker, E. 1966. *Social Contract: Essays by Locke, Hume and Rousseau*. London: Oxford University Press.

Bright, Stephen B. 2003. The accused get what the system doesn't pay for. In *Prison Nation: The Warehousing of America's Poor*, edited by Tara Herivel and Paul Wright. New York: Routledge.

Chemerinsky, E. 2003. Three strikes: Cruel, unusual and unfair. *Los Angeles Times*, 10 March.

Cole, D. 2000. Why so severe? Tough-on-crime policies burden a disempowered minority. *Fulton County Daily Report*, 21 January.

Crawford, C. 1973. *Civil Disobedience: A Casebook.* New York: Crowell.

de Tocqueville, Alexis. [1835] 1994. *Democracy in America.* New York: Knopf (distributed by Random House).

Delattre, Edwin J. 1996. *Character and Cops: Ethics in Policing,* 3rd ed. Washington, DC: AEI Press.

Delgado, Richard, and Jean Stefancic. 2001. *Critical Race Theory: An Introduction.* New York: New York University Press.

Human Rights Watch. 2002. *Race and the Criminal Justice System: Summary and Recommendations.* New York: Human Rights Watch. Accessed at http://www.hrw.org/us/usdom.php.

Kelman, S. 1996. *American Democracy and the Public Good.* Fort Worth, TX: Harcourt Brace College Publishers.

Kennedy, Anthony. 2003. Annual American Bar Association speech, 9 August. Accessed 20 March 2005 at http://www.humanrights first.org/us_law/inthecourts/ABA_2003_Meeting_Justice_Kenne dy.pdf.

Kerner Commission. 1968. *Supplemental Studies for the National Advisory Commission on Civil Disorders.* New York: Praeger.

King, Martin Luther, Jr. 1964. *Why We Can't Wait.* New York: Signet Classics.

Knepper, P. 2003. *Explaining Criminal Conduct: Theories and Systems in Criminology.* Durham, NC: Carolina Academic Press.

LeMay, M.C. 2000. *The Perennial Struggle: Race, Ethnicity, and Minority Group Politics in the United States.* Upper Saddle River, NJ: Prentice Hall.

Lewis, M. 1993. *The Culture of Inequality,* 2nd ed. Amherst: University of Massachusetts Press.

Liptak, Adam. 2004. Study suspects thousands of false convictions. *New York Times,* 19 April.

Locke, John. [1690] 1967. *Two Treatises on Government.* Cambridge: Cambridge University Press.

Owen, Robert. 2003. Absolute power, absolute corruption. In *Prison Nation: The Warehousing of America's Poor,* edited by Tara Herivel and Paul Wright. New York: Routledge.

New Journal, 2005. Felons Rights Court Abdicates Duty to Fairness. *New Journal.* 15 November.

Patterson, Orlando. 1991. *Freedom in the Making of Western Culture.* New York: BasicBooks.

Rawls, John. 1971. *A Theory of Justice.* Cambridge, MA: Harvard University Press.

Reese, Renford. 2004. *American Paradox: Young Black Men.* Durham, NC: Carolina Academic Press.

Ropers, Richard H., and Dan Pence. 1995. *American Prejudice: With Liberty and Justice for Some.* New York: Insight Books.

Russell, Katheryn. 1999. Critical race theory and social justice. In *Social Justice/Criminal Justice: The Maturation Of Critical Theory In Law, Crime, and Deviance,* edited by Bruce A. Arrigo. Belmont, CA: West/Wadsworth.

Walton, H., Jr., and C.C. Smith. 2000. *American Politics and the African American Quest for Universal Freedom.* New York: Longman.

Washington, Booker T. [1901] 1995. *Up from Slavery.* Oxford: Oxford University Press.

Wood, Daniel B. 2004. California tackles its prison problem. *Christian Science Monitor,* 20 July.

Zinn, Howard. 1968. *Disobedience and Democracy.* New York: Random House.

Chapter 2

The Race Card

America first played the race card when it enslaved millions of Africans to ensure economic prosperity. In the aftermath of slavery, America still engaged in this callous and unsympathetic exercise. In order to understand the attitudes and behavior of contemporary U.S. policymakers in the context of race and the criminal justice system, it is important to retrace the policies of their progenitors. The legacy of racially discriminatory policies in one form or another is one of the distinct features of American life. The federal government's glaringly delayed reaction to the black victims of Hurricane Katrina in New Orleans opened old, racially sensitive wounds. Moreover, the hypothetical suggestion of former U.S. Education secretary and national drug czar William Bennett that aborting all black babies would reduce the crime rate in the U.S. is reflective of a lingering and deeply troubling mindset.

An American Dilemma

The U.S. continues to follow a historical trend of confining black men by any means necessary. In *Why We Can't Wait*, Martin Luther King Jr. describes the travails of the black man in America.

> In the days of slavery, this suppression was openly, scientifically and consistently applied. Sheer physical force kept the Negro captive at every point. He was prevented from learning to read and write, prevented by laws actually inscribed in the statute books. He was forbidden to associate with other Negroes living on the same plantation, except when weddings or funerals took place. Punishment for any form of resistance or

complaint about his condition could range from mutilation to death. Families were torn apart, friends separated, cooperation to improve their condition carefully thwarted. (1964, 13)

After the abolition of slavery, the advent of other forms of bondage was a precursor to a pattern of public policies that would affect the African American throughout American history. The **black codes** of the Southern states—postwar legislation intended to limit severely the rights of blacks—were so restrictive that they amounted to barely camouflaged bondage. Those enacted and enforced in Mississippi, for example, prohibited blacks from leasing or renting land outside of town limits, effectively thwarting their efforts to become independent farmers. The legislature of South Carolina restricted blacks from occupations other than farm labor or domestic service. In other regions of the South blacks were required to get written permission from their employers in order to leave the plantation (Royce 1993, 67). In these cases, slavery had been only slightly modified.

Some thirty years after emancipation, between 1890 and 1920, in response to perceptions of a "New Negro" born in freedom, undisciplined by slavery, and unschooled in proper racial etiquette, and in response to growing doubts that this new generation could be trusted to stay in its place without legal and extra-legal force, the white South denied blacks a political voice, imposed rigid patterns of racial segregation (Jim Crow), sustained an economic system—sharecropping and tenantry—that left little room for ambition or hope, refused blacks equal educational resources, and disseminated racial caricatures and pseudo-scientific theories that reinforced and comforted their racists beliefs and practices. (Allen et al. 2000, 11)

From 1866 to 1877, during the period known as Radical Reconstruction, the North attempted to force the South to put the nation's egalitarian principles of democracy into practice. During this period of reform, blacks had an unprecedented degree of political access. Indeed, blacks sat in political offices at the national, state, and local levels (Trefousse 1971, 58). The first Civil Rights Act was passed in 1866, guaranteeing all persons, non-whites as well as non-citizens, the same legal rights as white citizens (Tompkins 1995, 132).

Efforts to democratize American society continued with the passage of the Fourteenth and Fifteenth Amendments in 1868 and 1870. The Fourteenth Amendment contains the equal protection clause, prohibiting any state from depriving "any person of life, liberty, or property without due process of law, nor deny[ing] any person within its jurisdiction the equal protection of the laws" (Tompkins 1995, 132).

The Fifteenth Amendment gave black men the right to vote. It prohibits the federal government and the states from denying or abridging the right to vote based on race, color, or previous condition of servitude (Schmidt et al. 1999).

Many public policies that ostensibly helped liberate blacks have been revealed to be little more than mirages. Most of the progress made between 1866 and 1876 towards civil rights quickly evaporated with the 1876 presidential election of Rutherford B. Hayes. Southerners pledged their support for Hayes only after they were guaranteed the termination of Radical Reconstruction, which was considered to be a form of martial law imposed on the Southern states by the North (Blumberg 1984, 6). Although Samuel J. Tilden won more popular votes than Hayes, Hayes prevailed in this controversial election. Because the North was forced to compromise in the Hayes election, it reneged on its promise to rearrange Southern society so that it would be representative of America's egalitarian creed (Myrdal 1944; Dye 1995).

The Fourteenth and Fifteenth Amendments carried little weight in the South. The brief enfranchisement of blacks ended in 1877 with the inauguration of Hayes and subsequent segregationist laws. The activities of the Ku Klux Klan and other terrorist organizations ensured that blacks in the South were not equally protected under the law. Although they maintained de jure voting rights, their de facto voting privileges were effectively nullified by the implementation of black codes and terrorist practices.

The legal system sanctioned white supremacy and favored the rights of whites over the rights of blacks. In the South, terrorist organizations like the Klan existed outside the law, and discriminatory practices flourished within the law. Some of the legal maneuvers that effectively disenfranchised blacks included the **white primary**. Whites were the only people allowed to vote in primary elections. The U.S.

Supreme Court upheld this practice until 1944 when, in the case of *Smith v. Allwright*, the Court found that it violated the Fifteenth Amendment. The **grandfather clause** restricted blacks from voting unless they could prove their grandfathers had voted prior to 1867. **Poll taxes** required voters to pay a fee to vote, thereby excluding most blacks, who were too poor to pay. These taxes were not outlawed until the ratification of the Twenty-fourth Amendment in 1964. **Literacy tests**, which required voters to read, recite, or interpret complicated texts such as a section of the Constitution, also restricted the right of the black population to vote. Local registrars were left in charge of determining who passed and who failed (Schmidt et al. 1999).

The Fourteenth Amendment, ratified in 1868, states, "No State shall make or enforce any law which shall abridge the privileges or immunities of citizens of the United States … nor deny to any person within its jurisdiction the equal protection of the laws." This amendment ostensibly protected blacks from discrimination and seemed to be a gallant effort by the U.S. to harmonize its society. In the 1896 landmark case *Plessy v. Ferguson*, however, the U.S. Supreme Court ruled that laws requiring blacks to use separate railroad facilities were not at variance with the Constitution. The Supreme Court inverted the interpretation of the Fourteenth Amendment, stating that the amendment's equal protection clause did not prevent state-enforced separation of races (Dye 1995; Tompkins 1995). In *Plessy v. Ferguson* the Court's interpretation of the equal protection clause of the Fourteenth Amendment stated:

> The object of the [Fourteenth] Amendment was undoubtedly to enforce the absolute equality of the two races before the law, but in the nature of things it could not have been intended to abolish distinctions based upon color, or to enforce social, as distinguished from political, equality, or a commingling of the two races upon terms unsatisfactory to either. Laws permitting, and even requiring, their separation in places where they are liable to be brought into contact do not necessarily imply inferiority of either race to the other … (Dye 1995, 47)

The Supreme Court reflected the will of the people. Jim Crow laws separating blacks from whites continued to perpetuate segregation in the South (Blumberg 1984). It took American society 58 years—from 1896 to 1954—to realize the concept of "separate but equal" was unjust, unconstitutional, and undemocratic.

The misuse of the Fourteenth Amendment has been one of the most problematic aspects of the U.S. judicial process. Current criminal justice statistics show disparities in the system supporting the conclusion that not all U.S. citizens enjoy equal protection of the laws.

The impact of World War II on race relations in the U.S. was dramatic and exposed the glaring contradictions between the U.S. domestic and international agendas. Abroad, the U.S. claimed to be the destroyer of evil and the protector of democracy. At home, however, it was neither. Black organizations initiated a "Double Victory" campaign to urge the federal government to prevail against social injustice abroad and at home. The crisis created by World War II simultaneously brought blacks hope, opportunity, and despair (Kelley and Lewis 1996).

The contradictions of American society are vividly highlighted in the autobiography of the great black educator and theologian Howard Thurman. In 1935, Thurman was invited by the national YMCA and YWCA to be the head of a four-person delegation that would travel to India, Burma, and Ceylon. The general goal of the trip was to spread goodwill and understanding about the Christian faith. After Thurman's first lecture at a law college in Colombo, Ceylon, the chairman of the department approached him. The man stated, "I had not planned to ask you this, but after listening to your lecture I am convinced that you are an intelligent man. What are you doing here?" The man reminded Thurman of the contradictory and ironic nature of his Christian-oriented message. The department chairman stated, "Your forebears were taken from the west coast of Africa as slaves, by Christians. They were sold in America, a Christian country, to Christians. They were held in slavery for some two hundred years by Christians ... since that time you have been brutalized, lynched, burned, and denied most civil rights by Christians." The man goes on to tell Thurman of a poignant story he read in a U.S. newspaper.

> I read a clipping from one of your papers giving an account of how one in your community was being hunted down by a mob on a Sunday night. When the men in a nearby church

heard the news they dismissed the service and joined in the manhunt. When the poor man had been killed they went back to resume their worship of their Christian God. (Thurman 1979, 14)

Many terrorist activities have exposed the contradictory nature of American society. Few race-inspired tragedies, however, have had a greater transformative impact on U.S. society than the Emmett Till case. The brutal 1955 murder of 14-year-old Till horrified thousands of blacks and motivated them to participate in the struggle for civil rights. Till was brutally beaten and killed for speaking "fresh" to a white woman in Money, Mississippi. The woman's brother and husband found Till, beat him, gouged out one of his eyes, shot him, tied him to a cotton gin, and threw his body into the Tallahatchie River. In the trial, an all-white jury found the defendants not guilty (Reese 2004).

Over the years, an array of strategies have been employed in the U.S. to control the black population. Slavery was the first and most inhumane form of control. Later, other acts of racial brutality would send the clear and grim message that blacks should know their place and not tinker with their inferior status. Lynching became the most frightful and grisly form of intimidation.

The book *Without Sanctuary: Lynching Photography in America* traces the history of lynching in the U.S. According to its authors, lynching was a response to the emancipation of the slaves. It rose from fear of black progress, a taste for "folk pornography," and even boredom (Allen et al. 2000, 13). Lynching was not only accomplished by hanging. This vigilante form of punishment by death without due process of law was also carried out by burning, shooting, stabbing, or whatever other means were at hand, so long as the result was maximum suffering.

> To kill a victim was not enough; the execution became public theater, a participatory ritual of torture and death, a voyeuristic spectacle prolonged as long as possible (once for seven hours) for the benefit of the crowd. Newspapers on a number of occasions announced in advance the time and place of a lynching, special "excursion" trains transported spectators to the scene, employers sometimes released their workers to attend, parents sent notes to school asking teach-

ers to excuse their children for the event, and entire families attended, the children hoisted on their parents' shoulders to miss none of the action and accompanying festivities. (Allen et al. 2000, 13)

In the 1890s, an average of 139 people were lynched each year, 75 percent of them black. The number of lynchings declined in subsequent decades, but blacks accounted for 90 percent of the victims. Between 1882 and 1968, an estimated 4,742 blacks were killed by lynching (Allen et al. 2000, 2).

Whether it is the tacit endorsement of terrorist practices such as lynching or through legislative agendas, creative ways to punish black men have always existed in the U.S. Society has unremittingly embraced policies that attempt to control the black man. State-sponsored capital punishment has replaced lynching as the ultimate punishment for violent behavior. The use of the death penalty in the U.S. also has racial overtones that expose disparities in the U.S. criminal justice system.

In 1967, the President's Commission on Law Enforcement and the Administration of Justice stated that the death penalty in the U.S. reflected discriminatory patterns. "The death penalty is disproportionately imposed and carried out on the poor, the Negro, and members of unpopular groups." In 1982, the National Minority Advisory Council on Criminal Justice found that the imposition of capital punishment was the most instructive example of the disparities in the criminal justice system. In 1987, the American Society of Criminology publicly condemned capital punishment as a racist tool. They urged professionals in their field to use their voices to denounce the practice (Baker 2003, 177).

The various players in the criminal justice system have used their discretion to impose the death penalty. The subjectivity of their judgments in capital cases has led to widespread disparities. Prosecutors play the most important role in the capital sentencing process. Indeed, they are the primary culprits. While many critics are quick to blame politicians and judges for being insensitive to black males, there is not a group in the U.S. that has been proven to be less sensitive to black males than prosecutors. Prosecutors, many with aspirations to become judges and politicians, have exacted an incalculable toll on the black community. It is their unchecked discretion in the criminal justice system and their lack of sensitivity that has helped to punish, humiliate, demean, and control a significant population of black men. Prosecutors are responsible for deciding whether to seek the death penalty in a particular case. They build their reputations on being tough on crime, and the decision to execute an offender is an example of their toughness. To prosecutors, killing a black man who is found guilty of a heinous crime is a win-win scenario. They sustain their bravado and build an aura of toughness when they execute an individual for whom society has no compassion.

> Prosecutors are directly responsible for determining whether charges will be brought against offenders, what the specific charges will be, and if plea bargains will be proffered. The immense power of the prosecutorial position also extends to jurisdictions with grand juries, where prosecutors are commonly in charge of choosing the witnesses to be called, questioning the witnesses, interpreting the law, and making recommendations to the grand jury regarding cases. Furthermore, neither the accused nor the legal representative of the accused may be in attendance, and information about the proceedings is denied to the accused and his/her legal counsel as well as the public. (Free 2003, 138)

After the prosecutor outlines the sentencing scheme, judges and juries decide this life or death matter. All parties come into the courtroom with certain racial prejudices, and it is in the courtroom that these prejudices are made manifest. How else can one account for the woefully disparate capital sentencing over the years?

In the 1930s the federal government began keeping records of state-sanctioned capital punishment. Since that time, 5,000 people have been executed by state and federal jurisdictions. Of this total, 2,200 have been white and 2,300 have been black. On the surface this seems proportional; but it is not, when the population percentages of blacks and whites are taken into account. Blacks have made up about 12 percent of the U.S. population but account for 52 percent of those executed. Whites have hovered around 82 percent of the general population and make up 47 percent of those executed (Baker, 2003, 179).

Between the reinstatement of capital punishment in 1976 and April 1, 2003, there were 842 executions carried out in the United States. The following data from *Death Row USA*, a quarterly report by the Criminal Justice Project of the NAACP Legal Defense and Education Fund, suggest that blacks are significantly more likely than whites to get the death penalty. They also suggest that the death penalty is more likely to be imposed if the victim is white.

Capital Punishment in the U.S.
Top number = year, Bottom number = executions

77	78	79	80	81	82	83	84	85	86	87	88	89	90
1	0	2	0	1	2	5	21	18	18	25	11	16	23

91	92	93	94	95	96	97	98	99	00	01	02	03
14	31	38	31	56	45	74	68	98	85	66	71	22

Gender of Defendants Executed
842 total executions

Female	10	1.19%
Male	832	98.81%

Gender of Victims
1271 total executions

Female	623	49.02%
Male	648	50.20%

Race of Defendants Executed
842 total executions

White	447	56.65%
Black	290	34.44%
Latino/a	56	6.65%
Native American	13	1.54%
Asian	6	0.71%

Race of Victims
1271 total victims

White	1022	80.41%
Black	174	13.69%
Latino/a	50	3.93%
Native American	3	0.24%
Asian	22	1.73%

The Willie Horton Effect

D.W. Griffith's 1915 film *Birth of a Nation*, based on *The Clansman, an Historical Romance of the Ku Klux Klan* by Thomas Dixon, Jr., helped to solidify whites' fear of the "dangerous and savage" black man. The theme of this film revolved around miscegenation. No other issue in America was as explosive as interracial mingling. This film played on the fears that whites had regarding what they perceived to be the overly sexual, undisciplined, and primitive black man. The climax of the film showed the "noble" KKK galloping to save humanity from the on-slaught of black savages. It was the KKK's capacity to control the wild

Defendant-Victim Racial Combinations

	White Victim	Black Victim	Latino/a Victim	Asian Victim	Native American Victim
White Defendant	448 (52.02%)	12 (1.43%)	6 (0.71%)	3 (36%)	0 (0%)
Black Defendant	182 (21.62%)	87 (10.33%)	10 (1.19%)	7 (0.83%)	0 (0%)
Latino/a Defendant	28 (3.33%)	2 (0.24%)	22 (2.61%)	1 (.12%)	0 (0%)
Asian Defendant	2 (0.24%)	0 (0%)	0 (0%)	4 (0.48%)	0 (0%)
Native American Defendant	12 (1.43%)	0 (0%)	0 (0%)	0 (0%)	1 (0.12%)
Total	672 (79.81%)	101 (12.00%)	38 (4.51%)	15 (1.78%)	1 (0.12%)

Note: In addition, there were 15 defendants (1.78%) executed for the murders of multiple victims of different races. Of those, 8 defendants were white, 4 were black, and 3 were Latino.
Source: NAACP Legal Defense and Educational Fund, *Death Row USA*, 1 April 2003.

and aggressive black man that made them heroes. This film became recruiting propaganda for the KKK and other terroristic organizations.

Birth of a Nation was the most profitable film of its era. It was king of the box office for more than two decades, grossing $18 million from 1915 to1935. Because of its cinematic innovations, *Birth of a Nation* became one of the most important films in American history. It also remains one of the most controversial, not because of its cutting-edge cinematic techniques, but because of its gruesome and brutally negative depiction of blacks. The NAACP vehemently denounced this film as racist propaganda. It was banned in eight states. The film was the impetus for riots that broke out in various cities in the U.S. After reviewing the film, President Woodrow Wilson is reported to have stated that it was "like writing history with lightening and my only regret is that it is all terribly true." For President Wilson, the 28th President of the United States, to endorse the authenticity of *Birth of a Nation* shows the depth of racial insensitivity that has existed in the U.S. (www.filmsite.org).

That racial bias and fear of blacks is still engrained in U.S. society nearly a century after the release of *Birth of a Nation* is illustrated by the case of Willie Horton. The Horton case represents one of the most insensitive distortions of facts in American politics. It is a sad and tragic episode in the media coverage of American Presidential politics. In the mid-1970s in Massachusetts, William Horton was convicted as an accessory to a felony murder for his part in a robbery. Joseph Fournier, a gas station attendant, was stabbed 19 times. According to authors Kathleen Hall Jamieson and Paul Waldman, there was no direct evidence that Horton killed Fournier and no evidence that the victim was tortured. There was some evidence, however, that Horton was in a getaway car doing herion during the time of the murder. Nevertheless, Presidential candidate George H.W. Bush, who changed William's name to Willie, to sound more black and menacing, alleged that "Willie Horton was in jail, found guilty by a jury of his peers for murdering a seventeen-year-old kid after torturing him." Bush operatives "whispered" to the media that Horton had cut off Fournier's genitals and stuffed them in the victim's mouth. This was a total distortion of the facts in which the press never challenged because they enhanced a powerful narrtive that is embedded into white America's psyche (Jamieson and Waldman 2003, 2–3).

Horton was sentenced to life in prison without possibility of parole. After serving eleven years, however, Horton was given ten weekend passes as part of the Massachusetts prison rehabilitative furlough program. During the two days he was out of prison on one of his passes, Horton kidnapped a young white couple. He stabbed the man and raped the woman. He did not murder either victim. Bush stated that Horton was allowed to murder again.

Michael Dukakis was the liberal governor of Massachusetts who had supported the state's furlough program. In the 1988 presidential election, Dukakis was the Democratic nominee against Republican

George H. W. Bush. It was a tough campaign for Bush. Many said he lacked vision, energy, and enthusiasm. The turning point in the Bush campaign came when his strategists held focus groups with so-called Reagan Democrats in Paramus, New Jersey. The meetings were designed to help Bush fine-tune his campaign message. Initially, the people in the group had a favorable opinion of Governor Dukakis; but as the focus group leaders began to ask leading questions, this favorable opinion evaporated. The Bush operatives portrayed Dukakis as being far to the left of the mainstream. For example, they asked the participants in the focus group the following question: "How would you feel if you knew that as governor of Massachusetts, Dukakis had vetoed legislation requiring teachers to say the Pledge of Allegiance at the beginning of the school day?" The group's reply was, "not so good." The focus group moderators also asked: "What about Dukakis's record on crime? During his term of office, Dukakis's prison administration had released on furlough a convicted black murderer named William Horton. While free, the inmate had brutally raped a white woman and terrorized her husband." The group also responded negatively to this information. The Bush operatives had provided the focus group with information about Dukakis that left them with extremely negative feelings about the Democratic nominee. The Bush team used the Willie Horton story in a television campaign to paint Dukakis as an ultra-liberal. Bush campaign director Lee Atwater would later boast to party officials, "By the time this election is over, Willie Horton will be a household name" (www.insidepolitics.org).

The Bush campaign alleged that Dukakis created the furlough program. This was false. Dukakis inherited the furlough program from his Republican predecessor (Jamieson and Waldman 2003, 2–3).

In the fall of 1988, Bush's election team constructed one of the most effective ads in the history of U.S. presidential campaigns. The television ad was called "Bush and Dukakis on Crime." It became known as the "Willie Horton ad." The following is the text of this ad:

> Bush and Dukakis on crime [*picture of Bush and Dukakis with text of Bush & Dukakis on Crime*]. Bush supports the death penalty for first-degree murderers [*picture of Bush with text of Supports Death Penalty*]. Dukakis not only opposes the

death penalty, he allowed first-degree murderers to have weekend passes from prison [*Dukakis picture with text of opposes Death Penalty, Allowed Murderers to Have Weekend Passes*]. One was Willie Horton, who murdered a boy in a robbery, stabbing him 19 times [*picture of Willie Horton, with text of Willie Horton on screen*]. Despite a life sentence, Horton received 10 weekend passes from prison [*picture of Horton under arrest by police with text of Horton Received 10 Weekend Passes from Prison*]. Horton fled, kidnapped a young couple, stabbing the man and repeatedly raping his girlfriend [*picture of Horton under arrest by police with text of Kidnapping, Stabbing, Raping*]. Weekend prison passes. Dukakis on Crime. [*picture of Dukakis with text of Weekend Prison Passes; Dukakis on Crime*]. Political message paid for by National Security Political Action Committee. (www.insidepolitics.org)

In the closing weeks of a lackluster campaign, the Bush team made Horton the poster child for tolerance by liberals of violent crime. The ad played to the fear of the savage black man that has always gripped the white population in America. Many say it was Bush's adroit exploitation of the Horton issue that won him the 1988 election and point to the complicity of the media in this race-baiting exercise.

Since 1988 many have sought to deconstruct the infamous Willie Horton ad and examine the reasons for its explosive power. Why did it resonate so thoroughly with the American public? Their analyses disclose the central theme of white America's fear of crime and its consistently perceived culprit, the black man. John Edgar Wideman candidly sums up the meaning of the Willie Horton ad:

> Willie Horton's Negro face, represented in a thuggish mug shot so he appears as the archetypal black rapist, assaulted voters with a sobering brutal message. No, the American Dilemma ain't solved yet. The black **other** of your worst dreams is still out there folks, just as wild, savage, dangerous and deviant as ever. What America needs, declared the ad, is a President who will keep this dangerous nigger in his place, lock him up forever or execute him—not a liberal like Mike Dukakis who, as governor of Massachusetts, paroled Willie Horton, thereby allowing the black brute to rape again. (Wideman 2003, 33)

Demonization of the Other

In the late 1980s and early 1990s, everyone wanted to get tough on crime. The crack epidemic took its toll on urban communities. During this period the public clamored for more police protection and safer streets. Politicians responded to these cries by creating tougher laws against offenders. Many of these laws have turned out to be irrational and counterproductive. Very few politicians during this period were discussing the protection of civil liberties and civil rights. The universal message of politicians was to get tough on crime by any means necessary.

The Willie Horton episode marked the end of an era when liberal politicians openly fought for just and fair criminal justice practices. Horton was an albatross around the neck of Dukakis. Since Horton, politicians have not wanted to gamble on appearing soft on crime. In the 1990s, murder rates decreased by 20 percent while the coverage of murder increased by 600 percent (Glassner 2002). Overall crime rates decreased significantly while fear of crime continued to increase. Why? Because the media and politicians have created the fear of the **other**.

The U.S. has been notorious for its phobia of certain populations. As Michael Moore points out in the 2002 documentary *Bowling for Columbine*, when Americans look abroad, their anger, fear, and hatred is directed toward Muslim populations. Domestically, Americans have directed the same emotional fervor towards the black male. As Moore states, "one thing you can always count on is white America's fear of the black man." The media have been complicit in this black-male-phobic exercise.

Probably the most important fear conditioning that is accomplished by TV programmers, however, is the implicit association between violence and minorities, especially African Americans. The repeated pairing of minorities with fearful circumstances on television cannot help but create highly negative and largely unconscious memories associated with groups such as blacks and Hispanics, and the existence of these implicit memories can only serve to strengthen racial and ethnic stereotyping and perpetuate racism. (Glassner 1999)

For their comprehensive study on youth, race, and crime in the news, Lori Dorfman of the Media Studies Group and Vincent Schiraldi of the Justice Policy Institute examined stereotypes and misconceptions that are fueled by the media. According to their study, some 76 percent of the public state that they form their opinions about crime from what they read and see in the news. Their study concluded that 86 percent of white homicides are committed by other whites; and overall, whites are three times as likely to be victimized by other whites as by minorities. The probability that a white will be the victim of a crime by a black youth is small. Moreover, African Americans are underrepresented in news reporting as victims and overrepresented as perpetrators. Articles about white homicide victims tend to be longer and more frequent than articles about African American victims (Dorfman and Schiraldi 2001).

Race Cases

The issue of race is a ubiquitous element of life in the United States, and the public is now accustomed to the race card being played in several settings. Various high profile cases in recent years have highlighted the problematic issue of race more than others, however. One example is the 1989 case of Charles and Carol Stuart.

On October 23, 1989, Carol Stuart—the pregnant wife of Charles Stuart—was shot in the head and Charles was shot in the abdomen. Charles told the police that a black assailant forced them to drive to the Mission Hill area—a predominantly black neighborhood in Boston—where he robbed and shot them. Doctors performed an emergency Caesarean on the wounded Carol Stuart, who died the next day. Her newborn died a couple of weeks later. Some 100 officers searched for the alleged black perpetrator. A suspect was found in the person of 39-year-old William Bennett. Charles Stuart picked Bennett out of a police lineup, saying he recognized the shape of Bennett's ear. There were glaring inconsistencies in Stuart's recollection of what happened that tragic day. However, this did not deter authorities from pursuing the alleged black assailant.

A little more than two months after the shooting, Charles Stuart's brother and his friend told investigators that they were unwitting accomplices in a plot contrived by Charles to kill his wife. The Suffolk County District Attorney ordered the arrest of Charles Stuart for the murder of Carol Stuart. One day after his hoax was revealed, Charles committed suicide by jumping off a bridge. A $100,000 life insurance policy on Carol Stuart was found at the couple's home the next day (*Boston Herald* 1991, 008).

Historically, black men have faced a circus of stakeholders eager to mete out punishment for alleged criminal activities. Indeed, the players have been the police and the sheriff, the judges, prosecution, witnesses, jury, and media. This formidable team of opponents has made it very difficult for blacks to receive justice, fairness, and equitable treatment. The Charles Stuart case is reflective of a legacy of injustices enthusiastically embraced by many sectors of U.S. society. Although the various elements of the criminal justice system have played a role in entangling black men, in the past two decades politicians have been among the most active players in this race-phobia game. Their knee-jerk complicity in playing the race card has been deeply troubling.

For example, just two days after the Stuart shooting, Massachusetts state Republicans urged lawmakers to pass a capital punishment bill. The mayor of Boston rebuked them for using the Stuart case for political exploitation. The state Republican chairman, however, maintained that public support for the death penalty was not a partisan issue. He went on to add, "While we feel pain and sympathy for the victims of this crime, all of us feel anger and outrage at their brutal assailant and at a criminal justice system that seems to care more for the rights of criminals than the rights of innocent victims of crime" (Phillips 1989, 16). The intensity of Republicans' outrage in response to this case was palpable. What specific population in U.S. society can arouse such intense hatred? These lawmakers were sure the assailant was black. This justified their anger and their reflexive call for capital punishment.

The most troubling aspect of U.S. society is that we do not learn from past mistakes. We do not challenge our stereotypes vigorously enough. We believe our gut instincts are right all the time. But even gut instincts can be socialized. Many Americans have been conditioned to fear the black man and to take any means necessary to control him. Perhaps this mode of thinking has become a self-fulfilling prophecy for some black men. If you tell a person they are crazy for a lengthy period of time, they will begin to act out the label given to them.

The 1994 Susan Smith case is another high-profile race case that aroused raw anger and emotions throughout white America. Five years removed from the Stuart case, the Smith case stirred the same types of emotions, anger, and finger-pointing. Because it allegedly involved the death of two white children at the hands of a black assailant, the case quickly garnered national attention. It was seen as a serious threat to social order. Susan Smith claimed that an armed black man had kidnapped her two young boys near Union, South Carolina. Smith was allegedly forced from her car at gunpoint by the black man. As she pleaded with the carjacker to free her kids, the man sped away with her two little boys still strapped into their car seats. The case was the impetus for collective white outrage and sorrow. The grieving mother's description of the perpetrator led law officers to search for the culprit among young black men in six states.

But this case turned out to be the racial hoax of hoaxes. Smith later admitted to driving her kids into a lake. As one Chicago man stated, "I guess she figured if she said a black man did it people would believe her no matter what kind of story she came up with. That's what hurts. As long as it's allegedly a black man involved, America will fall for anything" (Terry 1994, A16). A white school psychologist from Mount Pleasant, South Carolina, candidly summarized the sentiments of many. She stated, "Smith had chosen the right colored monster to generate the most sympathy and fear for her plight, especially in the hearts of white Americans." She continued, "It did make her story seem more likely. I wouldn't like to think we're all prejudiced, but I guess there's that typical profile of the old, bad black guy. We're just too ready to accept that" (Terry 1994, A16).

Smith's life was spared for killing her two children. Would this have been the case if her story were true and authorities found the black thug who kidnapped her toddlers? Would his life have been spared? Would psychiatrists and analysts have delved into the man's past and explained his irrational behavior as being the result of familial dysfunction that included a father who committed suicide, a messy divorce, and sexual exploitation? Would these factors be feasible in sparing the life of a black man who killed two white kids? There is little doubt that the black perpetrator of the type of act alleged by Smith would be the victim of capital punishment. Indeed, the death penalty is reserved for special cases such as this. Herein lies the contradictory and hypocritical nature of the U.S. criminal justice system. It is based on a false, skewed, and distorted sense of equity, fairness, and justice.

The Smith case is one of the periodic "us" versus "them" cases in the U.S. The initial cries of "Look what you people did!" opened old wounds and increased the distance between blacks and whites in several regions of the U.S. But the instinctual nature of Americans to blame the black man for crime and violence permeates every rung of American society. When politicians embrace the same debilitating stereotypes and have the same knee-jerk responses to the racialized perceptions of criminal activity, there is a fundamental problem that muddies the complexion of U.S. society. James Madison, in Federalist 10, envisioned politicians as being representatives of the people pursuing the common good—sophisticated individuals who could remain above the fray and the self-serving interests of the ordinary citizen.

Newt Gingrich, formerly the Speaker of the House of the U.S. Congress and once one of the most influential politicians in the nation, was rebuked by Vice President Al Gore for statements he made regarding the Susan Smith case. Gingrich stated that "the case vividly reminds every American how sick the society is getting and how much we have to have change." He continues, "the only way you get change is to vote Republican" (*New York Times* 1994, A20). Gingrich's sentiments reflected the mindset of an increasing number of mean-spirited and callous conservatives who pressed for harsher sentencing and a punishment-only philosophy for inmates. Conservatives of his ilk ironically professed vision when dealing with offenders but lacked the foresight to confront the consequences of reintegrating non-rehabilitated inmates into society. A bigger tragedy is that conservatives on the far right of the ideological spectrum influenced liberals to embrace a similar mindset and similar remedies for offenders; e.g., harsher punishments, fewer educational and recreational programs in prisons, and more emphasis on punishment than on rehabilitation.

I once asked a correctional officer what the purpose of the prison system was. He responded by saying, "The system exists not to punish or to rehabilitate." I was puzzled by this response. I asked him to elaborate. He stated, "We warehouse. That's what we do." According to this correctional officer, it was not the duty of the prison to provide rehabilitation; it was the responsibility of the inmate.

There has been a callous and insensitive philosophy embraced by many decisionmakers in the context of prison rehabilitation. For example, the Federal Prison Industries Competition in Contracting Act proposes to restrict inmate training and employment in federal and state prisons. Initiatives that propose to restrict educational opportunities and recreational activities for inmates have also gained momentum over the last decade. Every day some 1,600 inmates are released from prison. What purpose is served by restricting them from preparing for life after prison? If you deny inmates education and training in prison, how will they be prepared for reintegration into society? How will these policies reduce recidivism?

It is shortsighted to put the onus of rehabilitation squarely on the shoulders of the inmate. Does it make sense only to punish, or in the words of the correctional officer, warehouse inmates if the goal is their successful reintegration into society? Where is the vision? Where is the foresight when it comes to criminal justice policies? In the late 1980s and early 1990s there was an enormous proliferation of prisons and prison inmates. What policymakers publicly contemplated the impact of incarcerating so many young men, mostly minority, on their communities and families? The negative ripple effect that incarceration has had on minority communities has been devastating.

There have been few attempts in the political sphere to examine comprehensively the familial and socioeconomic impact of punish-only policies on the black perpetrators of violent crimes. Thorough analyses seem undervalued by politicians who prefer simple solutions to complex problems. Can one imagine a more simple response to the complex problems of drug possession, theft, and gang violence than, "Let's lock them up and throw away the key"?

Building more prisons has become the solution *du jour* of both conservative and liberal politicians. Even Bill Clinton, the so-called first black president, was complicit in the political exercise of "locking them up and throwing away the key." Astute political observers will note that Clinton did what he had to do for the Democratic Party. He could not afford to return to the days of Dukakis. He did not want to gamble on sabotaging the party by appearing to be soft on crime, so he did the opposite. He endorsed policies that led to an unprecedented increase in the number of prison inmates. Because of Clinton's affability, the visibility of African Americans in his cabinet, his liberal stance on other policy issues, his familiarity with black church hymnals and ability to clap on beat, the black community gave Clinton a free pass when it came to the policy area that impacted their community the most.

According to a 2001 report entitled *Too Little Too Late: President Clinton's Prison Legacy*, the Clinton era experienced a quadrupling of the prison population. Some 8.5 million people were either under the control of the correctional system or working for the criminal justice system. This includes 2 million people working in corrections, 2 million people behind bars, and another 4.5 million on parole or probation. African American males were most affected by increased incarceration rates from 1980 to 1999. The rate for African Americans tripled, from 1,156 per 100,000 to 3,620 per 100,000 (Feldman et al. 2001).

Racial Disparities

In the U.S. criminal justice system, race significantly affects the probability that a person will be convicted of a crime. Race also determines the severity of the punishment. Blacks receive on average six months more in jail time than whites for comparable crimes (National Urban League 2004, 1). There are racial disparities among black and Hispanic inmates versus white inmates in every state in the union. Discrimination based on race violates the creed of the U.S. Constitution; more specifically, it violates the equal protection clause of the Fourteenth Amendment. This unattractive feature of American democracy represents a significant violation of human rights.

In his landmark book, *An American Dilemma: The Negro Problem and Modern Democracy*, Gunnar Myrdal poignantly discusses America's dilemma involving what to do with the black population. "There is a 'Negro problem' in the United States and most Americans are aware of it, although it assumes varying forms and intensity in different regions of the country and among diverse groups of the American people. Americans have to react to it, politically as citizens and, where there are Negroes present in the community, privately as neighbors" (1944, xlv). The question then was whether whites could peacefully and comfortably coexist with this population. In every period of American history, this has been the predominant theme. Perceptions and stereotypes of young black men as being lawless and dangerous have remained strong and consistent throughout the country's history.

In the 1950s, when segregation was legal, African Americans made up 30 percent of the nation's prison population. Today, they make up 49 percent of all prison inmates but only 12.6 percent of the general population. One out of every four black men aged 16–26 has some connection with the penal system; e.g., in prison, in jail, on parole, on probation. The federal government predicts that one of every four black men will be imprisoned during their lifetime (Reese 2001; Reese 2004). Waquant puts these startling statistics in perspective, when he says the incarceration of young black men in the U.S. "has escalated to heights experienced by no other group in history, even under the repressive authoritarian regimes and in Soviet-style societies" (Hallett 2003, 39).

What is the difference between the hyper-punitive, inequitable criminal justice policies of today with their emphasis on incarceration, and the black codes implemented in the South after the Civil War? The Jim Crow laws that existed in the South for more than fifty years? From a historical perspective, how has America changed its views of black men? The comments made by Martin Luther King Jr. more than four decades ago still resonate today.

> Jailing the Negro was once as much of a threat as the loss of a job. To any Negro who displayed a spark of manhood, a southern law-enforcement officer could say: "Nigger watch your step, or I'll put you in jail." The Negro knew what going to jail meant. It meant not only confinement and isolation

from his loved ones. It meant that at the jailhouse he could probably expect a severe beating. And it meant that his day in court, if he had it, would be a mockery of justice. (1964, 15)

Today, the U.S. is incarcerating an entire generation of black men. This trend is having a significant impact on black communities. Those incarcerated do not have jobs, pay taxes, or care for their children. Many cannot vote. "Felony disenfranchisement" restricts approximately four million Americans—mostly minorities—from voting. Because 45 states have laws restricting offenders from voting and 32 states deny those on parole the right to vote, at least one of every seven black men cannot vote, at least temporarily. Some 31 percent of the black men in Florida and Alabama are prohibited from voting because of felony convictions. On the national level, 13 percent of black men are disenfranchised because of felony convictions, compared to 2 percent of whites (Reese 2004; Cole 2000, 17A).

The opportunities for many young blacks to engage in full citizenship are restricted. In order for a democracy to thrive, all citizens must have the opportunity to engage in the various aspects of public life. As Kelman states, "Democracy recognizes the dignity and worth of each person ... by authorizing the lowliest as well as the mightiest to participate in governing, our government publicly affirms the value of every human" (1996, 7). The unequal treatment of young black men in the U.S. betrays the fundamental principles of democracy.

Lawmakers should reevaluate counterproductive criminal justice policies that lack vision, compassion, and practicality. Those who commit crimes should be punished. However, the punishment should always be proportional to the crime. The mean-spirited policy of "lock them up and throw away the key" might be expedient and useful to politicians, but it is not a long-term solution to the problem of crime in this country. More emphasis should be put on preventing crime by addressing its causes. More focus should be put on rehabilitating offenders so they can successfully reintegrate into society. Lawmakers should direct money into educational and recreational programs for youth, especially in areas acutely affected by crime. We must remember what Cesare Beccaria stated in 1764, because it rings true today: "It is better to prevent crimes than to punish them. That is the ultimate end of every good legislation" (Knepper 2003, 36).

Race and Incarceration in the United States
Rates of incarceration in adult correctional and confinement facilities per
100,000 state residents, by race

	White	Black	Hispanic	Ratio, Black/ White	Ratio, Hispanic/ White
Alabama	373	1,797	914	4.8	2.4
Alaska	306	1,606	549	5.2	1.8
Arizona	607	3,818	1,263	6.3	2.1
Arkansas	468	2,185	1,708	4.7	3.7
California	487	3,141	820	6.4	1.7
Colorado	429	4,023	1,131	9.4	2.6
Connecticut	199	2,991	1,669	15.0	8.4
Delaware	361	2,500	330	6.9	0.9
District of Columbia	46	768	260	16.5	5.6
Georgia	544	2,153	620	4.0	1.1
Hawaii	173	577	587	3.3	3.4
Idaho	502	2,236	1,103	4.5	2.2
Illinois	216	2,273	426	10.5	2.0
Indiana	373	2,575	602	6.9	1.6
Iowa	300	3,775	923	12.6	3.1
Kansas	397	3,686	753	9.3	1.9
Kentucky	466	3,375	2,059	7.2	4.4
Louisiana	421	2,475	1,736	5.9	4.1
Maine	207	1,731	759	8.4	3.7
Maryland	282	1,749	230	6.2	0.8
Massachusetts	204	1,807	1,435	8.9	7.0
Michigan	357	2,256	951	6.3	2.7
Minnesota	197	2,811	1,031	14.3	5.2
Mississippi	353	1,762	3,131	5.0	8.9
Missouri	402	2,306	730	5.7	1.8

	White	Black	Hispanic	Ratio, Black/ White	Ratio, Hispanic/ White
Montana	358	3,120	1,178	8.7	3.3
Nebraska	226	2,251	824	9.9	3.6
Nevada	630	3,206	676	5.5	1.1
New Hampshire	242	2,501	1,425	10.3	5.9
New Jersey	175	2,509	843	14.3	4.8
New Mexico	311	3,151	818	10.1	2.6
New York	182	1,951	1,002	10.7	5.5
North Carolina	266	1,640	440	6.2	1.7
North Dakota	170	1,277	976	7.5	5.8
Ohio	333	2,651	865	8.0	2.6
Oklahoma	682	4,077	1,223	6.0	1.8
Oregon	488	3,895	777	8.0	1.6
Pennsylvania	281	3,108	2,242	11.1	8.0
Rhode Island	199	2,735	817	13.8	4.1
South Carolina	391	1,979	871	5.1	2.2
South Dakota	440	6,510	1,486	14.8	3.4
Tennessee	402	2,021	790	5.0	2.0
Texas	694	3,734	1,152	5.4	1.7
Utah	342	3,356	998	9.5	2.9
Vermont	183	2,024	799	11.1	4.4
Virginia	444	2,842	508	6.4	1.1
Washington	393	2,757	717	7.0	1.8
West Virginia	375	6,400	2,834	17.1	7.6
Wisconsin	341	3,953	863	11.6	2.5
Wyoming	740	6,529	1,320	8.8	1.8
National	**378**	**2,489**	**922**	**6.6**	**2.4**

Figures calculated on basis of U.S. Census Bureau data from Census 2000 on
state residents and incarcerated population.
Source: Human Rights Watch 2002.

References

Allen, James, Hilton Als, John Lewis, and Leon Litwack. 2000. *Without Sanctuary: Lynching Photography in America*. Santa Fe, NM: Twin Palms Publishing.

Baker, David V. 2003. The racist application of capital punishment to African Americans. In *Racial Issues in Criminal Justice, The Case of African Americans*, edited by Marvin D. Free Jr. Westport, CT: Praeger.

Blumberg, Rhoda Lois. 1984. *Civil Rights: The 1960s Freedom Struggle*. Boston: Twayne.

Boston Herald. 1991. Chronology of events. 21 October.

Cole, David. 2000. Denying felons vote hurts them. *USA Today*, 3 February.

Dorfman, Lori, and Vincent Schiraldi. 2001. *Off Balance: Youth, Race, and Crime in the News*. Justice Policy Institute (April).

Dye, Thomas R. 1995. *Understanding Public Policy*. Englewood Cliffs, NJ: Prentice Hall.

Feldman, Lisa, Vincent Schiraldi, and Jason Ziedenberg. 2001. *Too Little Too Late: President Clinton's Prison Legacy*. Justice Policy Institute. February.

Free, Marvin D., Jr. 2003. Race and presentencing decisions: the cost of being African American. In *Racial Issues in Criminal Justice, The Case of African Americans*, edited by Marvin D. Free Jr. Westport, CT: Praeger.

Glassner, Barry. 1999. *The Culture of Fear: Why Americans are Afraid of the Wrong Things*. New York: BasicBooks.

Glassner, Barry. 2002. In *Bowling for Columbine*, a film by Michael Moore released in 2002.

Hallett, Michael A. 2003. Slavery's legacy? Private prisons and mass imprisonment. In *Racial Issues in Criminal Justice, The Case of African Americans*, edited by Marvin D. Free, Jr. Westport, CT: Praeger.

Human Rights Watch. 2002. Race and incarceration in the United States. *Press Backgrounder*, 22 February.

Kelley, Robin, and Earl Lewis. 1996. Introduction. In *From a Raw Deal to a New Deal: African Americans 1929–1945*, by Joe William Trotter Jr. New York: Oxford University Press.

Kelman, Steven. 1996. *American Democracy and the Public Good*. Fort Worth, TX: Harcourt Brace College Publishers.

King, Martin Luther, Jr. 1964. *Why We Can't Wait*. New York: Signet Classics.

Knepper, P. 2003. *Explaining Criminal Conduct: Theories and Systems in Criminology*. Durham, NC: Carolina Academic Press.

Myrdal, Gunnar. 1944. *An American Dilemma: The Negro Problem and Modern Democracy*. New York: Harper and Brothers.

NAACP Legal Defense and Educational Fund. 2003. *Death Row USA*. Washington, DC: NAACP.

National Urban League. 2004. *The State of Black America*. Washington, DC: National Urban League.

New York Times. 1994. Vice President rebukes Gingrich for citing murder case. 8 November.

Phillips, Frank. 1989. GOP's death penalty call brings rebuke from Flynn. *Boston Globe*, 25 October.

Reese, Renford 1999. The socio-political context of the integration of sport in the U.S. *Journal of African American Men* 4, no. 3 (Spring).

Reese, Renford. 2001. Criminal justice and social injustice: African American men in the U.S. *Journal of Ethics and Justice* 3, no. 2 (November).

Reese, Renford. 2004. *American Paradox: Young Black Men*. Durham, NC: Carolina Academic Press.

Royce, Edward. 1993. *The Origins of Southern Sharecropping*. Philadelphia: Temple University Press.

Schmidt, Steffen W., Mack C. Shelley, and Barbara Bardes. 1999. *American Government and Politics Today*. Belmont, CA: Wadsworth.

Terry, Don. 1994. False accusations anger black people. *Times-Picayune*, 6 November.

Thurman, Howard. 1979. *With Head and Heart: The Autobiography of Howard Thurman*. New York: Harcourt Brace Jovanovich.

Tompkins, Jonathan. 1995. *Human Resource Management in Government*. New York: Harper Collins College Publishers.

Trefousse, Hans L. 1971. *Reconstruction: America's First Effort At Racial Democracy*. New York: Litton Educational Publishing.

Waquant, L. 2001. Deadly symbiosis: When ghetto and prison meet and mesh. In *Mass Imprisonment: Social Causes and Consequences*, edited by D. Garland. Thousand Oaks, CA: Sage.

Wideman, John Edgar. 2003. The American dilemma revisited: Psychoanalysis, social policy, and the socio-cultural meaning of race. *Black Renaissance* (Spring) 2003:33.

www.filmsite.org. The "Birth of a Nation." Accessed at http://www.film site.org/birt.html.

www.insidepolitics.org. Independent ads: the National Security Political Action Committee, "Willie Horton." Accessed at http://www.insidepolitics.org/ps111/independentads.html.

Chapter 3

The Life of an Inmate

Michael "Quake" Fisher, a black inmate at Centinela State Prison in Imperial, California, wrote me a two-page letter early in 2004 to tell me he enjoyed reading my first book, *American Paradox: Young Black Men*. He supported its thesis: that young black men have unwittingly embraced one model of black masculinity: the **gangsta thug**. The enthusiastic embrace of this model has manifested itself in counterproductive behaviors ranging from underachievement in school to street violence and criminal activities.

"Quake" was incarcerated for manslaughter in 1993, when he was 19 years old. In his letter, Quake expressed his desire to live a better life once he was released. He discussed how much he had grown mentally and spiritually while he was in prison. When I read his two-page letter, I knew instantly that he was a brilliantly insightful casualty of the false bravado that is so often embraced by young black men. He got caught up early in life in the macho, counterproductive, and self-destructive culture of gangs. Before Quake could truly understand the irrationality of his gang behavior, he was serving a 12-year sentence for manslaughter.

I met Quake in May 2004 when I visited Centinela State Prison to speak to a group of black inmates. I was there at the invitation of an educational representative at the prison, a beautiful spirit who has gone to great lengths to help rehabilitate many inmates. She had read my book and was responsible for passing it along to Quake.

The day I spoke at Centinela, it was 100 degrees in the shade in Imperial, which is southeast of San Diego, California, near the Mexican border. As I drove up to the prison gates, I saw a relatively modern facility, built in 1993, spread over an area of 2,000 acres. Though

I have spoken to many groups of inmates, I am always amazed at the utter night-and-day transition from the free world to the confines of a prison. I have never experienced a greater environmental contrast than that at Centinela.

I spoke to two groups of inmates that day. The first group was on Level 3—inmates incarcerated for violent crimes. On Level 3 there are individual cells, fenced perimeters, and armed coverage. The second group was on Level 1, known as "Easy Street." Level 1 inmates are incarcerated for nonviolent crimes or are awaiting parole. This level is characterized by open dormitories without a secured perimeter.

There were approximately twenty-five inmates in each group. While over the years I have spoken to more than a hundred diverse groups in various settings, I have never felt the emotional connection I experienced while speaking to the inmates of Centinela. I saw each of them as an extension of myself. At some point in my presentation to these men, I realized I was living the life they could have been living if they had had a healthy social and familial environment, received proper mentorship and guidance, and made better decisions.

After lecturing to each group of inmates for an hour about living a balanced, purpose-driven life, I opened the floor to discussion. In each group, inmates were eager to ask questions and engage me on an array of issues. This led to intense and emotional dialogues during the question-and-answer part of my presentation. Of all of the inmates who spoke up that day, Quake stood out as the most articulate, engaging, and insightful.

I vowed to mentor this young man and not let him fall through the cracks after he was released on parole in March 2005 at the age of 32. We began to develop a mentor-mentee relationship, and I gave him several writing assignments. As he completed them, I grew even more impressed with this young man's mind. His insights into prison life and culture were comprehensive and riveting. His analysis was intricate, nuanced, and poignant. I read some of his narrative to my father, who is a retired journalist, and he was impressed with Quake's writing as well as his ability to step back from his situation and interpret it. Most people cannot detach themselves from their immediate situation or environment. Very few have the analytical capacity to connect the dots and create new knowledge, make complex correlations and identify the causal relationships of a particular phenome-non. Quake has this ability. His summaries gave me a more solid un-derstanding of prison culture.

The following sections are the words of Michael "Quake" Fisher. They have been edited only for typographical errors. In these next pages, Quake candidly deconstructs prison life and culture in a way no scholar could, as he writes of inmate-guard relationships; race, gangs, and violence; self-improvement; state of mind; and relation-ships between inmates and female companions.

Inmate-Guard Relationships

Being that I have served so many years in prison, I have been ex-posed to so many different types of correctional officers. I really can say that I've seen them all—dealt with them all. If you were to ask an in-mate to describe a certain guard in just one word, more than likely they would use words like "asshole," "racist," "cool," or "sellout." Like I've said earlier, I have dealt with them all and over the last twelve years, I have had very little problems from them and they've received very little problems from me. The way I carry myself, the way I look, and the reputation I have, all play a part in why my relationships with most of them were "cool." If a guard seemed to show any signs of wanting to play games with me I would immediately tell them that there's too many inmates doing what they shouldn't be doing for you to be all in the face of an inmate trying to program accordingly. I also let them know that if they really choose to "go there," it won't be an outcome that they'd like one bit. I never been a shit starter but it's well-known that I'm a finisher. I refuse to be disrespected or touched by a guard. Those acts justify any counter acts I choose to partake in.

Guards are far from dumb. They know who to mess with and who not to. They know the inmates that are all mouth and they know the ones that have a violent streak in them. The more violent ones usually are the ones who are just trying to be left alone while they do their time. The loudmouths tend to be the ones always in guards' faces and crying foul when they find themselves in a jam.

Allow me now to explain exactly what makes guards fall into certain "types." The "cool" guard doesn't have to break any rules or shall I say cross the line in order to be liked. They may give you extra phone time, an extra tray of food, or extra recreational time. Of course, these privileges usually are given to inmates that carry themselves in a decent manner. A "cool" guard can also be one who has the attitude that they're here to just give their eight hours of work and leave. They may not give you anything other than what you have coming but they leave you alone and allow you to do your time. I know of some who sit at a podium for eight hours and read magazines. The only time they get out of their seat is to do count or pass out the mail, which both only take ten minutes total. The most important thing to me that makes a guard "cool" is when they treat you with respect and never come off seeming like they think they're better than you. Some even try and give you advice on how to go about getting prepared for that free world. A guard who shows concern about an inmate is the guard that gets a lot of love from most. Those guards are few though.

An "asshole" would be entirely opposite from the previous mentioned. They tend to bring a lot of their issues from home to work with them. Some seem to have more miserable lives than the incarcerated folks. Since misery loves company, they find working in a prison to be the most therapeutic place to be. They find pleasure in demeaning inmates. They harass inmates for the smallest infractions. They're sort of like the cop who patrols one of the most violent neighborhoods but spends most of his time writing the homeless tickets for begging. They seem to get a high off of telling inmates "no," whenever they're asked something. While other inmates set themselves up for failure, I refuse to ask them for anything. I'd wait for the next shift to come and hope someone less of an "asshole" is working that day. They purposely let you out for showers and phone calls late but are very punctual when it comes to wanting you to hang up or get out of the shower. All these acts are considered acts of a "lightweight-asshole" though. The "heavyweight" is the one that sits in the gun tower with an itchy trigger finger. The one who is more quick to pepper spray or hit an inmate with his club. The one who calls you a "bitch" or "punk," in hopes to get you to assault him so he can get a paid vacation.

Like I said before, they know who to mess with. They also know what institution they should work at. On maximum security prisons you won't find as many "assholes" as you would in a lower security prison. On a maximum, there are more inmates with life sentences, which equate to having "nothing to lose." On a lower security, you have more inmates with release dates. Obviously the inmate with a chance of one day being free will show more restraint when it comes to assaulting a staff member. That act will more than likely lead to a life sentence and guards are well aware of this. Them "asshole" tactics in a maximum security prison usually lead them to being stabbed and stomped out. They may get that paid vacation but they, more than likely, won't enjoy it because they'd be bedridden and in a lot of pain. There have been times when the "cool" guards have gotten together and had a few "assholes" transferred to other institutions because their rogue ways were even putting them in danger.

Now the "sellout" and "racist" is somewhat self-explanatory but allow me to show you how they receive such labels. If you're an "asshole" but only toward other races while showing favoritism toward your own then that might raise a red flag. Many Blacks are quick to accuse White guards and Hispanics of being racist. Sometimes the shoe fits and sometimes it doesn't. In any event there's not much you can do about it besides write complaints to their supervisors but you must understand that they all live in the same community and go to the same churches and parties. The odds of them taking an inmate's side over their employee-friend are slim to none. Your best bet is to just give the "racist" his space and don't allow him to turn yourself into a hate monger. You even have White guards that dislike their own race and favor the Black inmates. That leads to the guard being called a "nigger lover." They usually express this under their breath and behind closed doors. Hearing that word can lead to a race riot in a matter of minutes. I can recall a time when a White inmate was drunk and told to lock up by a White guard. He did lock up but he hollered out "Fuck you nigger lovers!" as the cell door was closing. Everybody was shocked. This was an inmate that didn't carry himself in such a way most White supremacists did. He had no tattoos of swastikas like most. Being that Blacks overwhelmingly outnumber the White population, a race riot was not in their best interest. The White inmates chose to discipline the inmate themselves in hopes it would deter from a riot. He also was forced to go door to door of all the Blacks and apologize. This issue was then laid to rest. So as you can see, guards that have their own issues with race can affect the race relations within prison.

I actually had all right relationships with some of the guards that were seen as the most "racist" and biggest "assholes" in most inmates' eyes. Once again this would confirm the fact that they knew who to mess with and who not to. I was applauded by many staff members for the way I carried myself and they also knew that I had influence on a lot of other inmates, specifically youngsters. I wasn't a "shot caller" but I was given the same amount of respect as one since I was considered one of the "realest niggas" incarcerated. I paid my dues, never would bow down to anyone, and had a criminal record that consisted of murder and attempted ones. Staff tries to use my kind and "shot callers" to their advantage. Instead of writing a lot of discipline paperwork up on an inmate, they'd tend to go ask one of us to just give the youngster a pep talk and show them the proper way of going about doing time.

There were times when a certain officer would cell search and confiscate bags of prison wine. They would then take it to their office and later allow an inmate they're "cool" with to steal it out the office. Some might think he's playing both sides but if you dig deep into it, you'd see it for what it really is. The inmate the guard gave it to would always sneak and give half back to the other inmate. The inmate who had got it confiscated, more than likely drew attention to himself that caused the search in the first place. He might have even been one of those that were known to act a fool when drunk so to alleviate any possible drama on the yard, it was taken away. The guard could have easily written up a disciplinary report on the inmate for manufacturing alcohol, which would have led to loss of privileges and more time added to his release date.

Rarely do Black guards participate in such activities. They're the last people on the payroll that are trying to lose their job. I guess it's like most Blacks even in the free world with jobs. They know they must perform to their best ability just to keep up with their White *counterparts. You'll find many White guards giving things and doing favors for White inmates and Hispanic staff doing the same for Hispanic inmates than you'd see a Black guard "looking out" for a Black inmate. Those Black inmates that don't understand the circumstances of the Black guards, tend to throw "sellout" and "house nigga" at them with the quickness. The instant they tell them, "No, you can't have a five minute phone call to tell your mother 'Happy Birthday'," they become them labels.*

Women guards come in all the same types as well. You tend to question why a woman would want to work in such an environment like a men's prison. Some see it as nothing more than an opportunity to financially support their family. Some seem to hate men and see this as a chance to get a slice of revenge by being an "asshole" in their own right. Females have had their share of being assaulted whether it was unwarranted or provoked by themselves. Some women come to work and are able to escape from the harsh free world for eight hours. Instead of at home where the husband pays them no attention, they get many men's undivided attention. Men who rarely get to interact with females like they would on the streets. A lot of unattractive and overweight White women get a lot of attention from the Black inmates. Since the superficial free society treats them like shit, they enjoy the compliments and gawking. They flirt and have a lot of conversations with inmates that include a lot of sexual innuendo. That's about as far as it goes but it will do for both sides.

Back in the late 80s and early 90s there were many romantic relationships between female guards and inmates, but due to inmates bragging about them, leading to investigations and firings, it has declined. There's only a few these days that go undetected. I have two associates that are both now married to former prison guards. Women come to work in tight uniforms that expose their panty lines and you have women that wear only loose outfits. Both are seen as making statements. You have females that don't wear a drop of makeup in an attempt to dress down. Then you have those that pour on the makeup and perfume as if they're headed to a club. You have White female guards who despise White inmates and show favoritism toward Blacks. You have Black female guards favoring the White inmates and despising the Black inmates.

Race, Gangs, and Violence

After watching several documentaries about the "prison gang culture" in states like Arizona and Texas, I was left amazed at how different they were in comparison to California's. Even the intelligence that the so-called "experts" have gathered on the "gang culture" in California's prisons is different from what it really is. Their intel is so outdated that one can't help but laugh when he sees an "expert" on TV trying to inform the free public about what goes on "behind the walls." The gangs that get the most mention, like the B. G. F. (Black Guerrilla Family) for example, are practically of non-existence. I honestly can say that I have never met an active member from that gang during the last twelve years of my incarceration. Being that I was once a very active player in the prison gang infrastructure at one point in time, I feel I have a better take on the situation than some professor from Georgetown University.

I made a quicker transition than most when it came to going from "Indian" to "chief," or the more commonly used terms, "soldier" to "shot caller." This was due to my street credibility and ironically, my intelligence. Most would say you had to even lack common sense to be in a gang so to be considered an intelligent gang member is sort of like an oxymoron.

Many individuals enter the pen with reputations of being "real niggas," "hard," and "killers," but a lot of them lose them labels over time—some quicker than others. One of the main reasons is because they no longer have them guns on their person that helped them build such a persona. Many come to find that them guns don't make you a man, nor does it give you a "real" heart or spine—just a false sense of having them. Truth be told, there are more people that are "playing the part" these days than those who are really "about it." Many these days join gangs out of peer pressure, wanting to fit in, and to get protection. Joining a gang is something they are really not feeling but they do it anyway. Back in the days, many were true hoodlums and yearned to live for it and die for it. Today, some attempt to keep up the act but eventually get exposed when shit hits the fan. Situations like race riots or when physical or verbal altercations amongst each other arises become tests of character. A "real" man, for that matter, would never allow someone to put their hands on them, take what is theirs, or call them out of their name, using words like "bitch" or "punk."

Unlike other races who enter the pen and choose to come together as a whole, the Black population has continued to struggle with such a concept. Hispanics have rival gangs amongst each other, as well as the Whites, but all issues are put to the side and they push "Brown Pride" and "White Power." They all partake in race riots unlike the Blacks. They also tend to have one "shot caller" calling the shots for all. That's another concept the Blacks don't feel as well. We tend to carry the view that "No nigga can tell me what to do." Clearly that's not entirely true since "shot callers" do exist in "cars."

I can recall a time when I first came to prison and the Hispanics were feuding with the Bloods. Ever chance they got, they would stab a Blood and we'd go back on lockdown. This same scenario happened for a year and a half. I was tripping on how the Crips wouldn't join in. I was only an Indian at the time so I couldn't make the decision to help. I knew the chiefs that could real well though. I'd ask why it isn't a Black thing like the Hispanics see it as a Hispanic thing and he'd say that the Bloods need to handle their own business before they ask for help. It just so happened that the Crips were the "realest" and "deepest" and if we were to get into it with the Hispanics, we'd crush them. The Hispanics knew this as well and loved the fact that we distanced ourselves from the Bloods. Only after a Hispanic stabbed a Crip that was standing near a Blood did the Crips decide it was time to do something. Assaulting someone near someone who's not involved is a violation in prison. The Hispanics knew now that the next go around we'd be joining in so they chose to stop attacking the Bloods. The beef was then over.

Here's an example of how clearly power is in numbers and how the Black inmate population continues to ignore such a fact, leading them to be victimized in such large amounts. Now first of all, I don't think we should come together just for the sake of violence. I would like this unity to be more based on putting an end to the violence we mostly inflict on each other on them streets. Being that the Hispanic population has more unity and must all roll with the protocol implemented by who many believe is the "Mexican Mafia." Blacks have the tendency to have more casualties in the violent race riots that occur frequently. Of the 400 Hispanics on a prison yard, 90 percent of them will partake in the event, where of the 200 Blacks on the yard, only 33 percent of them will be involved. Another 33 percent will be running for their lives and the other 33 percent will more than likely not even go to the yard when there's such a rumor running around that it may be "going down." This scenario has taken place over and over again all over prisons inside California. Not only do the Blacks have to deal with the fact they're outnumbered by Hispanics but they also must deal with the guard in the gun tower during a riot since nine out of ten times it will be a Hispanic or White guard with the finger on the trigger. Of course, they have the crosshairs on a Black male and not on one of their own. With so many people on the streets and in prison that are against Blacks, it's hard to understand why to this day, many refuse to throw in the gang-bang towel and start showing love for each other.

Of late, the "real" individuals have been ignoring where one is from and what he claims, joining together in the "game of survival." Many have come to find out the hard way that just because someone is from where you're from, doesn't mean they truly have your back. They also are starting to wake up and realize that there's more in life than this prison scene. When you're "real," you don't worry about what the next guy think so that allows you to distance yourself from the drama, seek education and most importantly, seek God.

With Black-on-Black crime so common on the streets, it amazes me how it's not like that at all in prison. It has extremely little to do with this newfound love for each other. It has more to do with the fact that guns are no longer available. It's hard to many to make that transition from AK-47 to a toothbrush with a razor blade at the end for a weapon. You still get a few stabbings here and there but nothing compared to the number of assaults the Hispanics inflict on each other—even the Whites. Unlike the streets, in here we're seen as the most civilized and the other races are seen as animals who don't know how to act. Many people have made excuses as to why it is the way it is because they hate the perception that without guns they ain't shit. Some say that the reason Hispanics and Whites trip so much is because they were already known for stabbing each other on the streets so it will only come natural even in here. *They also feel that the reason they get each other is because they have a large number of snitches and child molesters that must be dealt with. Then there's the drug drama over debts not being paid. There's truth to all these views but I still think that without guns on them streets, many Blacks would not be in prison. Hispanics know the risk of getting caught for a sticking is high but they do it anyway. We see that as Kamikaze. Blacks want to get away with shit and that's another reason they deter themselves from such acts.*

The only unity you're likely to get from the Black population is when they form "cars." Cars are a variety of different gangs from the same city or county that choose to now run together in prison. You have the Pomona car, the Long Beach car and so on. Being that the city of Los Angeles has so many gangs, they break theirs down by names and numbers. For example, all those that claim Rolling 60s, 40s, 30s, and 100s would fall up under what is known as the "0" car. Those that claim Hoover Street gangs all are, of course, in the Hoover car, just like all those from the "East Coast."

The Bloods do the same but are more united as one than the Crips as a whole. That has a lot to do with the Crips being seen as the "Big Man on Campus," which tends to always bring all the others together. San Diego has their Blood cars and Crip cars as well. The most interesting car to me would be the "IE" car, which is all the gangs (Bloods and Crips) from the Inland Empire. They usually won't have a "shot caller." They tend to run their car in a democratic fashion where everyone has a say and vote when it comes to making decisions like disciplining someone or bringing drama to another car. There's only one gang from Riverside, The East Coast 1200s, that roll with a LA car.

"Shot callers" tend to be the ones that have been involved in the gang longer and the ones with the hardest reputation. At least that's how it used to be. Nowadays, a scary dude can play that role if he happens to have money or a woman on his team that's bringing drugs in. With such leverage, he can somewhat buy power and control. He just needs to take care of the most aggressive gang members in the car. Keep them happy and willing to do the dirty work is the goal.

Another interesting fact about the gang culture inside here is the alliances between the Whites and the Hispanics and the Blacks and the "Others"(Asians). We share recreation areas with them as well as the showers, phones and dayroom. Rarely do these alliances team up to participate in violent activities against each other but it has been known to happen. The White and Hispanic alliance has a lot to do with the drug activity which involves a lot of using each other and extortion, both leading to a lot of inner fuming—especially behind debts. Both races also have another common ground, which is that they both hate and fear Blacks.

Being that we're both minorities you'd think if anybody was to join together it would be us Blacks and Hispanics but just like on the streets, we have allowed ourselves to fight over crumbs that the White race sets out on the table for us.

Like the White race, the Hispanic race has this crazy love-hate relationship going on with Blacks. You can walk down the tiers and hear these same Hispanics who hate us, playing our music loud through their speakers. They also run around speaking on the famous Black athletes and celebrities as if they're their best buddies, especially the late Tupac. I wonder if they would give Tupac a pass during a riot or would they get him too?

I myself have actually had quite a few good relationships with some Hispanics and some Skinheads. Like the guards, they also know who to mess with and who not to mess with—also, who to try and befriend. My reputation as being one of the "key figures" who walks prison mainlines allows me to receive the utmost respect from other races as well as from my own people.

Self-Improvement

When it comes to daily activities in prison, those in the free world tend to assume that there's not much an inmate can be doing in here. I so desperately wish that more inmates would prove them wrong instead of right. Over the years, I've seen many inmates go about "doing their time" in several different ways—some productive and most non-pro-

ductive. The rehabilitation process will only work if the person really wants it. There are a lot of opportunities available for the inmate to achieve things such as education and vocational trades. Just like those that take things like education for granted on the streets, you have double the number in prison. Many would rather waste their lives away playing board games and cards. I myself wasted many years in here by staying on them basketball courts and chasing Pruno (prison-made alcohol) and marijuana. I now am taking college courses with only a year left in my sentence but imagine if I would have been taking classes at least five years earlier. I'd really be ready for the free world if I had-of woken up then instead of now. I also earned me a couple of certificates in trades like A/C & Refrigeration but to have obtained more trades would of course been for my best interest.

The days of excuses and blaming the White man is so long gone. Playing the "poor me" game will get you nowhere in life. I had to check myself and realize I was better than this. I deserve better than this. I knew in order to stay out of these cells I'd have to prepare myself the best I can, mentally, physically and most importantly, spiritually. I refuse to be in that high percentage of repeat offenders.

These repeat offenders come in prison and do nothing until their name is called for release then when they come back, they cry about how hard it was out there on them streets—how no one is trying to hire them and what not. I have yet to see an inmate who has paroled after achieving degrees and trades while incarcerated, come back to prison. I really only know of a few who paroled so prepared for the obstacles they'd encounter on them streets.

Many inmates don't seem to wake up until they receive a life sentence. They begin to soul search. They begin to pick up the Bible, literature and open themselves up to a whole new outlook on life. Many would say that it's too late to try and change once you have a life sentence since you'll never be free, but it's never too late for a lost soul to find himself. It's never too late for someone to really learn what it is to be a man—also what it really means to be Black.

It's the knuckleheads that have all the release dates who continue to sleep—continue to gang-bang, smoke dope and just "kick it" while in prison. Many assume that they sit in cells and plot their next crime when they're set free but they're too lazy for even that. It doesn't take a lot of planning anyway to pick up a dope sack or gun once back in the free world. Even with knowing that whatever crime they commit, the consequences are not worth the prize, they still go out and do these silly "licks" that only amount to "crumbs," far from any real money.

It drives "lifers" crazy to see the same inmates come and go, continuously getting second chances. I'm so glad to be one of those with a date that plans to put my second chance to full use.

I thank God for giving whatever it was that allowed me to get up, get out, and get something. I also pray for there to be more like me who want to be part of the solution and no longer part of the problem. I'm not gonna be considered "job security" for these correctional officers and other law officials. They actually hate when inmates try and get on the right track by chasing education. They have shitty attitudes toward those teachers in prison that show they care about inmates wanting to change. That right there should be another reason for inmates to wake up. Basically, everyone needs a reason. I have many reasons for why I chose to switch my lifestyle up: for my mother, my son, my sister's kids who'll need a positive male figure in their lives since their father's a flop. Not only for those I do know I want to change for the better and help but also for those I don't know. Over the years I have found a lot of compassion within myself. I so desperately want to do my part in helping fellow brothers like myself bounce back. We all deserve better in life. We can bring a lot more to the table than being thugs, pimps, players and all that other bullshit that leads to incarceration and a lot of pain and stress for years.

I truly believe I was given this second chance for a reason. The DA and Judge can take all the credit they want for giving me a plea but I know God had his hand all over it. My attorney even said that the only reason they were willing to deal is because I only killed another Black, plus he was a dope dealer. If the victim was White, he said we'd be headed to trial without question. And of course, I would have been found guilty without question. I don't consider myself to be heavily religious nor do I pick up the Bible as much as I should, but I know without the little love I do receive from God, I wouldn't have been able to survive all these years in here. I could have gone in so many direc-

tions but He kept me stable—kept me sane. After entering prison and seeing so many with life sentences that did way less than the dirt I did on them streets, I knew I had been blessed. To screw up this blessing by not doing the right things when I paroled would to me be like a slap in God's face. We can't be having that. I'm so ready for them streets I can taste it. I want to show "The mainstream America" that we can change. More importantly, I want to show other brothers in prisons nationwide that regardless of the obstacles, our kind can make it happen. Even inmates in prison need role models.

This started off as an essay about daily activities but I got a little off track. As far as the actual daily activities go though, it clearly depends on the inmate. That's what I was trying to get at by writing that piece. The basic program would be to get up, go to breakfast then to school or work. Most just go through the motions, not really choosing to learn or build any work ethics they can carry out to the streets. Some don't have jobs, which means they'll get more recreation yard time to play basketball, handball, work out, gamble, get high, get in trouble or watch TV. The small percentage of those that are trying to get their lives right will limit all the previously mentioned activities and do a lot of reading, writing and taking college courses. They distance themselves from those that are content with underachieving in life. You actually have some that would like better for themselves but just don't have the ambition, the drive, and the will they need to take the steps required for such change. Laziness runs rampant inside these prison walls.

State of Mind

"A dumb nigga is a happy nigga." I can't recall where or when I heard that, nor who said it, but it has always stuck in my head. I didn't exactly know the meaning in it until I started my quest for change in life. I have now implemented my own take on the phrase. Walking these prison yards over the years, seeing different types of individuals, got me interested in wanting to know what goes on inside the next man's mind as he does his prison sentence. The ones who would interest me the most were the inmates who treated their stay in prison like

it was summer camp in a sense. Running around horseplaying all the time, thinking life is just one big game—never taking anything serious. You have some with life sentences talking about all they need is a smut magazine, a quart of Pruno and a couple dollars on their accounts and they're all right. Of all the things that life has to offer, these are the only things they say they need to suffice themselves. To many, the reality of things is hard to accept so they play and pretend a lot. They pretend that they're content with such unproductive lives until they die. The more they realize what really matters in life the more depressed they can get. Playing head games with yourself is a tactic many use to maintain mentally in here. Some smoke cigarettes and attempt to convince themselves that will relieve some of the stress. Some have other vices like writing females all day and talking to them on the phone every chance they get. Some bury their heads in that TV and of course, many run to drugs to help them cope with serving time. I feel that if you think small and set only small goals for yourself, you may be able to keep a smile on your face. I also think that deep inside they are going through a lot of misery and stress. Being that these things are perceived as signs of weakness in prison, many choose to act like all is good when it's not. I mean, how could you really be content with such a life when there's so much more you could be doing besides being stuck up in a damn cell day in and day out? When we start accepting reality and taking this struggle and strife head on there will be more of us not returning to this hellhole. Every time we're out there on them streets and think about committing a crime, we'll think about all that mental pain we once went through and don't want to deal with anymore. This place is enough to drive a sane man crazy if you let it. You can become institutionalized as well. The more I became aware of what's important in life, the more I became upset at myself for being in my current circumstances.

Family Relations

Family can play a pivotal role in an inmate's stay in prison. That support system is unlike any other. Homeboys and women can't com-

pare. It's sad that many are unable to have such a support system. Some only have themselves to blame. They have "burned bridges" by refusing to change their lifestyles whether it is a life as a gang-banger or dope addict. After many years of being in and out of prison, loved ones just get tired. No more sending financial support, and phones end up having blocks on them. No more visits, no more packages. Mothers tend to be the only ones on the family tree who don't turn their backs on you. It's funny to see all these dudes who thought they were "ballers" and "players" on the street, now be forced to turn to moms for money and things their "females" should be doing. Where's all their money from them dope deals? Where's all the females who were supposedly all over his jock? Some try not to use their mother for financial support and find ways to "hustle" inside these walls. It just don't seem right to some to beg from moms. Many though are somewhat spoiled and see no problem with it. They even call their mothers and have them use three ways to call girls who have blocks on their phones. They use their moms to chase down their baby mothers so they can come visit when mom does. Once an inmate comes up on a female, he tends to give his mother a break from sending money and running up her phone bill cause he's lonely and needs someone to talk to. So basically, the penitentiary is full of "Momma's Boys."

Some inmates do have love for their offspring and try to see them at visits. They write them and send them cards etc. Some use this as a ploy to get in good with their mothers but most, I would like to believe, are legit. Only problem is that when they get out, they lose this sense of truly wanting to be a father to their child because if they didn't they'd stay out of them streets and give them the proper love and support their children need, never returning back to prison, leaving them to fend for themselves. We tend to be mad that our fathers weren't around but we turn and do the same thing to ours, justifying our illegal acts as just trying to survive. Our kids would clearly be better off if we were to get an honest job and stay in the free world, by their side. Selling dope and buying them Jordan's with the money does not make you a good father. The truth is, many think it does make them one and when they get arrested, a few prison-made cards will keep the kid sufficed until free again. When one really learns what it means to be a father, he'll have a better chance at life on them streets.

Once he puts nothing above his children, he'll know that it's a must he stays out of prison for the kid's or kids' benefit. To make Momma proud can be another reason to get one's life on the right track.

I am blessed to have many family members still on my team and wanting the best for me when I parole. They are willing to help me get a place to stay and a place to work. Seeing so many others who lack this love and support allows me to be well aware of how blessed I am and how I'd be a damn fool to mess it up. I want to be able one day to return the same kind of love and support I was given during my darkest times. For me to be able to, I must get my life on the right track, which I have been doing for the last few years. Like I said at the beginning, family plays a pivotal role in one's rehabilitation.

Inmate-Female Companion Relationships

The prison culture promotes, get a female for all you can before she goes because without any question, she soon will. Women weren't seen as your better half but more seen as an accessory in your prison survival kit. There are those that do love their women but they actually don't know what it all means to love their women. In a heartbeat, they will write another woman if given the chance and just see someone new as a backup plan. I used that way of thinking to justify my wrongdoings. I have seen many inmates who had invested all their love in a woman and got abandoned. The stress it caused them was so catastrophic— you'd be a fool to do what he did. Men have always been more scared to set themselves up for failure by loving a female too much. Men also perceive love as a weakness so even if they do have it for a female, they downplay it, which also leads to a bad relationship. Females get the sense that their men worry too much about what others think.

Nowadays, you have many going online via family members and finding a lot of White women that are lonely, willing to correspond with an inmate. Black women are less likely to take this route to find a man. They tend to think that all a man in prison wants is a woman to send him packages and run up their phone bill. Most prison visiting rooms these days are filled with interracial couples. Many inmates run around the prison yards with photo albums full of fine sisters they were with on the streets but when they get out to that visiting room, their lady now is an overweight White woman who probably has some kind of dope sack on her person for him to take back to the prison yard. Most would assume that's the case always but there are those who just go out there to be in the presence of a woman. It gets lonely in prison just like it gets lonely in that free world for less attractive women. These unions work out for both parties. It's funny to see how Black women on the streets complain when a successful brother marries White, but there's little complaint to the rise in White women now forming relationships with brothers in prison.

Many inmates continue to treat these women who were there for them during hard times wrong once released, leaving many more women to be scorned and left feeling played. That has been the main reason Black women have deterred from dealing with brothers inside these walls. Each man campaigns how he's not like the others but they end up doing it too. Women tend to want a man in prison with long sentences (even life sentences). This way they don't have to worry no time soon about how he's gonna act once free. When dealing with a man in prison, a woman feels more needed by her man and she has someone she can write or accept collect calls from and tell all her problems to. She also doesn't have to worry about where he's at and who he's screwing behind her back. Even if some of the things she hears is not true, like how beautiful and sexy she is, it's still nice to hear and believe me, an inmate will give her a heavy dose of that.

Back to sisters for a minute—there are many who are down for their man like the White women but they tend to use a man's incarceration as an opportunity to now call shots they were unable to call on the streets. Inmates are willing to accept that in order to have a woman on their team though. Some sisters, although a small number, will take that risk of bringing drugs in so their man can send some of that money home to them to spend. I knew a female who had boyfriends at three different prisons and they all worked for her.

There are quite a few good relationships that exist between White women and Black inmates and Black women as well. I know a few *personally. I know a few inmates that got out and even married a few female correctional officers. So all inmates don't fall into the stereotype free society has put on them when it comes to them dealing with women. When one matures, he realizes that you should never hurt the one who was down for you, regardless if she doesn't look like Halle Berry. You also learn that it takes a good woman to help you stay on them streets and out of trouble. Womanizing, chasing women, is one of the main reasons brothers get caught back up in prison. Believe that.*

Chapter 4

Life of a Free Felon

America's correctional population includes more than 2 million prisoners, with another 4.7 million people on probation or parole. According the Bureau of Justice Statistics, no fewer than 6.9 million people are under the supervision of the nation's federal, state, and local prison systems. This represents 3.2 percent of the nation's adult population. There are more people incarcerated in the U.S. today than at any other period in our history, whether measured in numbers or as a percentage of the general population. The impetus for this startling increase is the "get tough on crime by any means necessary" philosophy embraced in the 1980s, which resulted in mandatory minimum sentences and longer sentences overall. While crime rates have remained steady or—in the case of violent crimes such as murder—fallen dramatically over the past decade, incarceration rates have continued to rise. Prison overcrowding is just one of many serious issues lawmakers must face as a result of espousing overly punitive, insensitive, and myopic policies. Others include the need for rehabilitation, reentry problems, and recidivism.

The Democratic presidential candidate John Kerry echoed the concerns of many regarding the alarming increase in incarceration rates when he stated, "I believe we have to stop being a nation content to spend as much as $50,000 a year to keep a young person in prison for life," at an Urban League meeting. He pointed out that the money would be better spent on educational initiatives (Usborne 2004, 25).

Taxpayer money over the past two decades has been spent on counterproductive and shortsighted punitive strategies to deal with offenders. Not enough money has been directed towards the prevention of crime. Since the 1980s, there have been twenty-one new prisons and no new universities built in the state of California. The more than $6 billion it costs each year to run the state's department of corrections exceeds the annual budgets of all California state universities combined. California has focused on punishment instead of prevention. These skewed priorities, mimicked in other states, have caused a crisis.

Inmate to Free Felon

Prison reentry is the process of leaving prison or jail and returning to society. All prisoners experience reentry irrespective of their method of release or form of supervision. So both prisoners who are released on parole and those who are released to no supervision in the community experience reentry. If the reentry process is successful, there are benefits in terms of improved public safety and the long-term reintegration of the former prisoner. Public safety gains are typically measured in terms of reduced recidivism. Reintegration outcomes would include increased participation in social institutions such as the labor force, families, communities, schools, and religious organizations. Successful reentry produces benefits for individual prisoners, their families, the communities to which they return, and the broader society. (Solomon et al. 2004, 11)

Once an individual enters the prison system they are entangled in a vicious and costly cycle. As Marc Mauer, assistant director of the Sentencing Project, states, "incarceration erodes job skills and reduces employment prospects, thus contributing to high rates of recidivism." There is a strong link between education and incarceration. According to Mauer, approximately 60 percent of black men who dropped out of high school serve time in prison by the time they reach their mid-30s. On any given day, 10 percent of the black male population under 40 is incarcerated. "Our bloated prison population of two million, costing about $57 billion a year, diverts both resources and attention from more constructive approaches to social problems like preschool programs, drug treatment and interventions with families at risk" (Mauer 2004, A18).

A 2005 study conducted by two Princeton University sociology professors, Devah Pager and Bruce Western, reveals the startling racial bias that is embedded in our society. They sent thirteen black, white, and Latino men posing as ex-convicts out in New York for over 3,500 interviews. Each participant's application stated they had been incarcerated for 18 months for a drug violation. The study found that in New York City, white men with prison records received far more offers for entry-level jobs than black men with identical records. Perhaps the most troubling finding was that white men with criminal records received just as many offers, if not more, than black men with no criminal records at all. "For every 10 white men without convictions who got a job offer or callback, more than 7 white men with prison records also did. But the difference grew far larger for black applicants: For every 10 black men without criminal convictions, only 3 with records got offers or callbacks" (von Zielbauer 2005, B1).

This study shows that four decades after the height of the civil rights movement, racial discrimination is still crippling the chances of black men to succeed in American society. The prospects for successful reintegration by black ex-offenders are even less hopeful. As New York City's corrections commissioner, Martin Horn, summarizes, "The world continues to be a very hard place for ex-offenders to succeed in ... and it's clear it's harder if you're a black ex-offender." Studies reveal that an employed ex-offender is far less likely to recommit a crime than one who is unemployed. Thus, as Horn states, the ability to find employment for ex-offenders "is every bit as important as putting more police officers on the street" (von Zielbauer 2005, B1).

In 2004, I was able to sit in on a parole hearing for an ex-offender named Garcia who had been incarcerated for various drug offenses. Garcia was married with two children. He had found gainful employment as a plumber since his last prison release. I was one of the five individuals at the parole hearing. The others were Garcia, his parole officer, a prison sergeant, and a commissioner who was the sole arbiter. Garcia entered the parole hearing room in an orange inmate jumpsuit and handcuffs. His parole officer alleged Garcia had committed four violations of his parole agreement: (1) failure to re-register his residence after ten days, (2) being in the vicinity of drugs, (3) possessing a dangerous weapon, and (4) obstructing justice. As I listened to Garcia, he seemed to have a legitimate explanation for each alleged violation, with many of his problems related to the fact that he was having an affair with a woman who did drugs. Garcia's defense for the first charge was that he left his mother-in-law's house, where he was registered, to stay in a hotel after getting into an argument with her. If a parolee is away from their registered residence for longer than ten days, they must re-register. Garcia said his clothes remained at his mother-in-law's house so he still considered that his residence. Garcia's defense for the second charge was that the woman he was having the affair with was a professional woman, and he did not know she was a drug user. The police did not charge him with being in the vicinity of drugs. As for the third charge, police found a table leg in Garcia's car trunk that was wrapped with duct tape and appeared to be a weapon. He said it was not his table leg and produced a letter from his wife, who said she put it in the truck to use it for a Mexican celebration involving a piñata. Regarding the fourth charge, when the police came to Garcia's lover's home, they knocked loudly on the door and then barged in. Garcia ran to hide in a bedroom. He explained his behavior as a knee-jerk reaction, one that could be expected of someone who was cheating on his wife.

I was convinced at the conclusion of Garcia's testimony that he would not be found guilty of any of the four violations and as a result would be released from custody. The commissioner told everyone to step outside for a fifteen-minute recess. I discussed the facts of the case with the prison sergeant and asked him what he thought. In response he immediately asked me for my opinion. I told him that all of Garcia's reasons seemed valid to me, and I would find him not guilty. The sergeant started laughing. He said, "I see you don't understand the system. It's set up for them to go back to prison. He will be found guilty of something." We returned to the hearing room and the commissioner announced he had found Garcia guilty on one count: possession of a deadly weapon. He was sentenced to serve twelve months in prison. It did not matter that what Garcia had in his trunk was a table leg wrapped in duct tape. It was not a knife, not a gun, but a stick. It did not matter that he had two young children and that his wife had written a letter explaining the table leg. It did not matter that Garcia had gainful employment. The sergeant told me that the system was unkind to offenders and once in the system, "you're pretty much stuck in the system." If what the sergeant said is accurate, then corrections departments are guilty of playing charades. They're guilty of playing the mean-spirited game of "Go back to prison."

An editorial in the *Houston Chronicle* summed up the problem with returning individuals like Garcia to prison for technical parole violations.

> The system should work to make communities safer. Instead, it sets up arbitrary obstacles that block petty criminals' reentry into productive society, all at an unduly high price to law-abiding taxpayers. Returning former offenders to a cell for minor technical violations wastes money that could be better spent on real anticrime solutions, such as substance-abuse treatment and remedial education. The current Texas system often turns one-time lawbreakers into hardened criminals and puts an intolerable strain on the prison system. Rather than playing gotcha with parolees and probationers, the Texas criminal justice system should make every effort to keep them out of jail while saving prison space for the real threats to society. (*Houston Chronicle* 2005, 10)

Merriam-Webster's Collegiate Dictionary defines a catch-22 as a paradox, "a problematic situation for which the only solution is denied by a circumstance inherent in the problem or by a rule." At every turn free felons face catch-22s that mean they will go back to prison. A newspaper article titled "They Want to Work" summed up the challenges facing free felons in its subtitle: "Sometimes the only thing standing between a job seeker and a job is the lack of a car or clothes or having a criminal record" (Joyner 2001, 1). Many free felons also lack the documentation required for employment. They do not have a birth certificate, a driver's license, or a Social Security card. Often, ex-offenders cannot get an apartment because many apartment complexes will not rent to felons. Our society wants free felons to walk the straight and narrow—but how can they, given the many obstacles? Who could?

It would be an interesting experiment to see how a recent Harvard graduate faced the same obstacles as a free felon. Let's say that graduating from the prestigious center of learning carries with it a debilitating stigma. Everywhere the recent graduate goes he is labeled as the worst element of society. No one trusts his judgment. No one trusts his motives. Take away his support network, including his family. Close his banking account and give him only $25 to live on after he leaves the university. Make him turn in his driver's license. Deny him an apartment or other housing. Tell him he must live in the same neighborhood he grew up in, but he cannot associate with the people who live there. Deny him gainful employment.

Do all this to a recent graduate of Harvard, and you dramatically reduce the probability that he will succeed in this society. In fact, you would likely have a scenario similar to the one in the 1983 classic film *Trading Places*. Dan Aykroyd, a successful commodities broker, and Eddie Murphy, a streetwise con artist, find their positions in life reversed as the result of a callous bet between two millionaires. Given all the perks and benefits of privilege, Murphy's character succeeds in his new life as a broker, while Aykroyd's character has an emotional breakdown in his new life as a destitute street person. Although comedic, this film is a powerful commentary on what might happen if a person with privilege is pushed to the fringes of society, to a place where they are forced to jump one hurdle after another while wearing ankle weights. Indeed, there is an important lesson to be learned from this film.

Attitude Surveys

In the spring of 2004, I surveyed ten inmates in an Incarcerated Youth Offenders (I.Y.O.) program at a California prison. This was not a random sample. The survey participants were enrolled in an educational program, which means they had already taken some initiative to get their lives on track. Without the rigor of a complex research study, I wanted to probe the mindset of these young men. The inmates were asked a range of five questions, two of which related to their current state and their future. Question No. 2 stated, "Describe prison life for you." Question No. 3 asked, "Are you positive or negative about your future? What are your plans for the future?" The following tables present responses to these two survey questions from six participants.

Age: 23
Hometown: Los Angeles, CA
Charge: Manslaughter

Describe prison life for you.

When dealing with individuals who need to rise above the influence of their emotions, I could never adjust to prison life. The majority of the people in the prison system are controlled by their emotions, mainly because they believe that they must follow them. At times it feels like I'm swimming in a sea of negativity.

Are you positive or negative about your future? What are your plans for the future?

I am very positive about the future. I have a solid plan set up that I will strictly follow. I know that there is nothing that can hold me back but me.

Age: 23
Hometown: Inglewood, CA
Charge: Robbery, 4 years

Describe prison life for you.

Depressing and educational. It has helped me realize that I no longer want to live a destructive life.

Are you positive or negative about your future? What are your plans for the future?

I am positive about my future sometimes and sometimes I'm unsure. I have many plans: (1) find employment ASAP, (2) start my own business, and (3) help others overcome this cycle.

Age: 27

Hometown: Fort Worth, TX

Charge: Robbery & Carjacking, 8 years

Describe prison life for you.

Prison life has really been a downfall for me. At the time in my life when I'm supposed to be adventurous, I'm here having to worry about the other men getting in my business. I'm used to only having to worry about my family's problems. It's real stressful being in here three states from home not having any family members close. Then this prison causes problems when I'm trying to deal with my family. Three or four times I had people come from out of state to get here and be denied a visit because I'm working or something. I try not to let people in here stress me out but from time to time they succeed because I let them.

Are you positive or negative about your future? What are your plans for the future?

I am not sure whether I am positive or negative for the future. Although I feel that I am more positive than I am negative. I know when my time comes I will come across something so I keep trying. I know my life purpose but I don't know what my career purpose is.

Age: 25

Hometown: San Pedro, CA

Charge: Armed Robbery, 9 years

Describe prison life for you.

Prison life for me has been a growing process. It has allowed a lot of things that I was involved in to come to a complete stop. Prison life has given me the opportunities to perceive life from a different vantage point. I mean I'm actually on the outside looking in. So I've had the chance to look into my life as it was. But it's given me a lot of time to figure out what I want my life to become. In the end, I think prison life has allowed me to gain knowledge over self and the power to control the things inside of me as well as outside of me.

Are you positive or negative about your future? What are your plans for the future?

I'm definitely positive about my future. I'm very optimistic about my plans for the future. Everybody's situation is different. I think a lot of my plans pertain to the well-being of my family. But I do have plans of opening up a small business in the near future.

Age: 25

Hometown: New Orleans, LA

Charge: Robbery, 12 years

Describe prison life for you.

Prison life for me has been stressful all the way around. I feel like a fish swimming in the sand of an arid desert. I'm out of my elements. The stressors of prison life are endless, the politics, the officers who abuse their authority, being deprived of your freedom and stress it put on my family. There's much more to it. It's very complicated.

Are you positive or negative about your future? What are your plans for the future?

I'm positive about my future because I've taken the necessary steps to make sure that I succeed. Failure is not an option. I plan on becoming a successful businessman. I've taken business classes in college and I've learned the basics of owning a business. For start-up money I'll probably try my hand at acting or modeling, a part-time job isn't out of the question. But, I refuse to come back to prison and have my freedom snatched again.

Age: 24

Hometown: Northridge, CA

Charge: Residential Burglary, 9 years

Describe prison life for you.

Too many people in such a small place—other's eyes are constantly on you. Either these people are nosy or bored. Sometimes it seems that you can never be alone. I guess I'm just tired with dealing in nonsense. I see me being a lot colder since I have been in here.

Are you positive or negative about your future? What are your plans for the future?

I am very positive about my future. I plan on keeping myself very busy with both school and work. First, I'm going to find a part-time position as a mechanic, at the same time I'm going to enroll in a community college and finish some courses then transfer to California State University, Northridge. I also intend to work on a little side project of mine, which is to design a company or a small business that will incorporate my artwork and other artists' works.

Challenges

As I walk around the prison yards, I can tell which inmates have a higher probability of reintegrating into society by their shoes. In the facilities I have visited, inmates can choose which shoes they will wear, and family members and friends can send shoes to them. If an inmate is wearing state-issued brown boots, it usually means he has no outside support. It is very difficult to succeed in the free world without support from family and friends. The system has proven to be unkind, and inmates cannot rely upon it to remove barriers to successful reentry. For example, in order to qualify for a job, a parolee needs a driver's license, a state identification card, or a Social Security card. Inmates who do not have healthy relationships with their families find it extremely challenging to get a birth certificate, the first step in the process of getting identification. In many prisons no assistance is given to inmates to help them secure the documents necessary for successful reintegration. By not taking this small step to help them reenter society, the prison system contributes to high recidivism rates. Instead of marking inmates for success, prisons become dream-killers.

Poet Langston Hughes asks, "What happens to a dreamed deferred? Does it dry up like a raisin in the sun or fester like a sore? Or does it eventually explode?" It is the nature of the human spirit to dream of a better plight. Inmates have dreams, too. Most of those I surveyed describe prison life as dark but saw their futures filled with light and potential. It is sad to see a dream deferred and tragic to see one killed. But politicians have become dream-killers. The sad reality is that the government is not on the side of inmates and not on the side of free felons. No matter how lofty their ideals and ambitious their goals, these inmates will face challenges that are almost insurmountable. When they realize their dreams are empty and that very few people are on their side, they will become embittered. Their rage and frustration will be taken out on a gang member down the street or a grocer around the corner. Herein lies the cause of the cycle of violence and dysfunction. One cannot aptly call this behavior self-destructive, because society and the government are key players in the destruction of the dreams of inmates and free felons.

Of course there are always exceptions. But statistics suggest the majority of those surveyed will falter. Unless they have the discipline to practice what they preach, support from their families and society, and help from the government, they are likely to return to prison.

Employment

In their responses about the future, there is some realism expressed by the survey participants. Most want to start their own businesses, perhaps because they know their prospects for being hired are slim. But employment is a condition of parole and probation. If they do not find jobs within a specified period of time, they violate their probation or parole. A slow job market at the time of their release is not taken into account. Nor is the fact that few companies hire freed felons. The irrationality of lawmakers and the rigidity of the system are both perplexing.

It is ironic, but true, that a felon has a better chance of being employed while incarcerated than he does when he is released. Another irony is that an illegal immigrant has a better chance of being hired than a free felon. This observation is not intended to demean illegal immigrants. It merely highlights contradictions in U.S. public policies. For example, while thousands of inmates struggle to find jobs when released from prison, in 2004 President Bush outlined a proposal to give temporary work permits to millions of illegal immigrants in the U.S.

In Georgia, there is a parole program that is a model of community support and supervision. Results Driven Supervision (RDS) identifies and addresses the four key elements associated with criminal behavior: education, substance abuse, criminal thinking, and employment. According to RDS, employment is crucial to an ex-offender's stability. Not only does it provide a means of legitimate income, it puts them in an environment of pro-social people—those who do not have a criminal mindset.

"I will maintain gainful employment." These words appear on the certificate of every parolee in the state of Georgia as a condition of their release. According to the Georgia Board of Pardons and Paroles (GBPP), "The importance and necessity for every able-bodied offender to find and maintain gainful employment is a basic condition for release from prison and a pro-social action that enables."

When parolees in Georgia are employed they are in the presence of law-abiding supervisors, or **capable guardians**. Criminal justice literature suggests that a person who is surrounded by pro-social thinking and capable guardianship is less likely to engage in criminal behavior than someone who is not. As GBPP accurately states, "Low education and job skills among many parolees, combined with a criminal record, present difficult obstacles to employment." They have created an initiative to help free felons overcome their employment hurdles. The Offender Parolee Probationer State Training Employment Program (TOPPSTEP) offers job skills training to offenders who are trying to reintegrate into society. According to GBPP, the parole staff is charged with collaborating with the Georgia Department of Corrections, the state Department of Labor, and businesses throughout Georgia to provide job opportunities for inmates (Georgia Board of Pardons and Paroles 2002).

Those involved with the TOPPSTEP initiative should be applauded for their willingness to do something about the serious problem of parolee employment opportunities. However, some critics charge that this program has fallen far short of its noble objectives. I interviewed a 42-year-old Georgia parolee about the challenge of finding employment. Frederick Steed's responses to me were candid.

Steed spent eight years in the Georgia state prison system for armed robbery. It was his first offense. He told me he got a job a few weeks out of prison because of his networking. He was employed only because of the people he knew. He stated, "Employment is king. It's the key to everything. It can make you or break you." Although it has always been difficult for parolees to find employment, the tragedy of September 11, 2001, made it worse. Employers began to require rigorous background checks. According to Steed, "Foreigners get less scrutiny than free felons." If employers discover a felony conviction in your history, they will not hire you. A good friend of Steed's got him a job at a Marshall's clothing store distribution center. There were only two blacks working there. The majority of the employees not involved in management were of Mexican descent. A raid on the facility revealed that the majority of the Mexican workers were illegal immigrants. Steed said it made him angry to see illegal immigrants getting jobs when free felons could not.

Institutional Mindset

Over time, prisoners can find comfort in the status quo. Inmates are socialized and conditioned by the prison system. The longer the prison stay, the more the inmate becomes familiar with the way of life there. Morgan Freeman's character in the film *Shawshank Redemption* poignantly illustrates how an inmate can become institutionalized. The predictable codes of prison culture and the strict regimen of prison life actually provide comfort to many. Indeed, the responses of inmates at a California state prison to my survey question—"Describe prison life for you"—cast light on how a person can become institutionalized in prison. For some young black men, prison life is all they know. One inmate who is 26 years old, born in Illinois, responds this way:

> In 1995, at the age of 17, I was charged with armed robbery and sentenced to six years in the California Youth Authority. I served five years and was released on parole. Five months later, I was charged with another armed robbery and sentenced to seven years. So between my 17th and 28th birthdays, I will only have spent five months outside of prison. Prison for me is like the very meaning of ironic. Though I would not wish it on no one, it has been an invaluable experience in my life. It has given me opportunities that I may not have otherwise utilized. (July 20, 2004)

The idea of surviving in the free world is daunting to many inmates. They know that the life of a free felon is filled with challenges, in the contexts of family relationships, living arrangements, employment opportunities, and the probation and parole process.

Reentry Support

Since I began speaking in prisons, I have received many letters from inmates. While the subjects are wide-ranging, many seek help and guidance when they are freed. One letter from an inmate in the California state system asked for my assistance in finding employment opportunities after his parole. There was nothing unique or remarkable about his letter; in fact, it was its plainness that caught my attention. It was representative of the general concerns of inmates who are approaching their release dates. I spoke at this inmate's prison on one occasion and remembered chatting with him. I did not know his crime and in our brief exchange, I could not gauge his sincerity about changing his life. However, his letter convinced me that he had at least some willingness to do what was necessary to reintegrate successfully into society. He had, after all, taken the initiative to write to me. Here is an excerpt from his letter:

> I made a decision to change the path I've been taking by enrolling in the prison's educational program. I've taken responsibility for my actions and now I'm going to move on with my life. I'm writing in hopes that you may be able to help me. I have family on the outside but we do not communicate on any level. There are no hard feelings towards them. I'm a man and it's time I begin my own life. I have fourteen months remaining on my prison sentence and would like to be productive when I'm released. You spoke of Black organizations on your visit with us and I was wondering if you are in contact with any of them that helps Black men who are soon to be released from prison find jobs, homes, and some kind of support group? I have a shaky past but I will not have the same future. Thank you for taking the time to read this letter. (May 16, 2004)

Here is part of the letter I wrote to this inmate in order to respond to his concerns:

In terms of black organizations that can help you reintegrate, there are many organizations and churches that have this as one of their written goals. Of course, as you know, many people do not practice what they preach. Let me know where you will parole and I will be sure to make some calls on your behalf. I definitely think that it is admirable that you want to start your own business. You have to be diligent and make incremental steps. When you get out you should strive to live a simple life. There is beauty and balance in simplicity. The more excess and variables you add to your life, the more drama you invite. When you get out you have to decide immediately who your friends are and who you can trust. My advice for you is not to kick it with anyone who is not positive, supportive, and forward-looking. I know this is an anxious time for you. Let me know your date for release. Also, let me know what types of jobs you are interested in. I have to convince an employer that you are worthy of a second chance. There are no guarantees but you have to be humble enough to take "any" type of job as long as it pays. Most of our millionaires started at the bottom with a legal hustle and a game plan.

I will put my neck on the line for you once. Do not disappoint me. You should use your incarceration as inspiration. My hero and idol Nelson Mandela spent 27 years in prison and came out a better man, not a bitter man. He used his time in prison constructively. (July 11, 2004)

In a second letter to me, this inmate expressed the frustration, fear, and desperation that many inmates must confront upon being released from prison. They know their crimes and subsequent convictions have pushed them to the fringes of society. They know that politicians despise them and society has given up on them. They know that it will be very difficult to make a successful transition because a full deck of cards is stacked against them.

I have had students throughout my teaching career who were fearful of life after college. The variables that cause this life-after-college syndrome are similar to those that cause the life-after-prison syndrome. Both the graduating student and the inmate who is being paroled are fearful of failing in life. Both groups are seeking gainful employment, a place to live, a means of transportation, and a support network. Students regularly e-mail me about how difficult it is to find a decent job to pay their bills. Increasingly, survival for university graduates is more challenging. If many of the nation's best and brightest young people are on the fringes of the job market, what are the prospects for recently released inmates?

While the graduating student worries about the lack of experience on their résumé, the inmate worries about having to check the convicted felon box on the application form. No crime other than political protests in an unauthorized zone can neutralize the requirement to put a check in that box. A conviction for robbery, burglary, theft, rape, or murder sabotages a person's application. Few people trust the convicted felon, or his judgment, temperament, or commitment. Many big-business owners are ideologically conservative. They are among those who have pushed for disproportionate sentences and espoused the kind of "justice" that advocates locking them up and throwing away the key. These are the people who insist that prisoners aren't entitled to educational opportunities while incarcerated. It is highly unlikely they will be enthusiastic about providing jobs for inmates.

Those who are felons and black find it particularly difficult to find meaningful, living-wage work when they are released from prison. It is challenging even for blacks who have not been involved in crime. Some progress has been made because of the civil rights movement, but significant disparities remain between blacks and whites where important social and economic indicators are concerned. For example, according to the National Urban League's 2004 report, *The State of Black America*, black unemployment is twice that of whites—10.8 percent versus 5.2 percent. In order to close this unemployment gap, 751,000 blacks would have to be added to the labor force. In addition, the report's "Equality Index" is a statistical measurement of the disparities between blacks and whites on key issues. The index establishes that the status of blacks is 73 percent of that for whites in terms of economics, education, social justice, health, and civic engagement (National Urban League 2004).

In 2004, the Legal Action Center (LAC) completed a comprehensive report on the legal barriers facing people who have criminal records. Their research found that ex-offenders seeking to reintegrate into society face "a daunting array of counterproductive, debilitating and unreasonable roadblocks in almost every important aspect of life" (Legal Action Center 2004, 1).

The LAC report points out that most legal barriers affecting reentry are state laws and practices. However, five significant federal laws have also had a debilitating impact. These restrict access to public assistance and food stamps (Personal Responsibility and Work Opportunity Act); housing (Housing Program Extension Act and Quality Housing and Work Responsibility Act); parenting (Adoption and Safe Families Act); mobility (Department of Transportation and Related Agencies Appropriation Act); and education (Higher Education Act). With the exception of the Higher Education Act—which bars those with drug convictions from student loans and other assistance—the states have flexible discretion in applying these restrictive federal laws. Because states can modify or override federal law in these areas, the LAC examined how each state chose to implement them. The following chart examines the policies adopted by California and Georgia in regard to driver's license privileges, employment, public assistance and food stamps, public housing, and voting.

The Legal Action Center 2004 Report
"What's the Law?"

California

Driver's License Privileges

1. Does the state revoke or suspend the driver's licenses of people convicted of drug-related offenses?

California passed a resolution on 12/20/2000 in opposition to enacting a law called for by the federal statute in order to receive certain federal highway funds. However, the state does revoke driver's licenses for drug-related offenses. Cal. Vehicle §§ 13202 and 13352.

2. If so, what crime(s) result in suspension or revocation?

Driving under the influence of alcohol or drugs and a range of drug-related offenses involving the use of a motor vehicle. Cal. Vehicle §§ 13202 and 13352.

3. If so, what is the length of the suspension or revocation?

The court shall determine the period of revocation or suspension for drug-related offenses. Driver's licenses will be revoked or suspended for 6 months to 5 years following a conviction for driving under the influence, depending upon the status of the offender, i.e., the number of times s/he has been convicted. Cal. Vehicle §§ 13202 and 13352.

4. Does the state offer restricted drivers' licenses for purposes of employment, education, and/or medical care?

If enrolled in a treatment program, an individual 21 years of age or older at the time of the offense and convicted once within a 7-year period of driving under the influence may obtain a restricted license for transportation to and from employment and/or treatment. Cal. Vehicle § 13353.7(a).

Employment

1. Can employers ask job applicants about arrests not leading to conviction?

No, with the two exceptions of law enforcement authorities and health care facilities (re: certain crimes), employers may not ask about arrests that did not lead to conviction or for which a pre-trial diversion program was successfully completed. Cal. Code Regs. tit. 2 § 7287.4(d)(1)(A), (B); Cal. Labor § 432.7(f)(1), (2); and Cal. Penal § 13203.

2. Can employers consider arrests not leading to conviction?

Yes.

3. Does the state have standards prohibiting employment discrimination by public employers and occupational licensing agencies based on a conviction record?

No.

4. Does the state have standards prohibiting employment discrimination by private employers based on a conviction record?

No.

5. Does the state restrict people with criminal records from employment in the field of home health care?

Yes. Applicants are barred from home health care employment for certain violent, sexual, and theft-related convictions (or similar convictions in other states) for an unspecified period of time, so the bar operates as a lifetime bar. Individuals with felony convictions can lift the bar with a certificate and expungement. The bar for misdemeanor convictions may be removed by expungement alone.

6. **After an individual has been convicted, does the state offer any mechanism to demonstrate that an individual has been rehabilitated?**

Yes, a Certificate of Rehabilitation that declares that an individual convicted of a felony is rehabilitated and may relieve an individual of registering as a sex offender. However, civil liberties are generally only restored by both a certificate and a pardon. In addition, while a certificate alone generally cannot remove occupational bars, it is a prerequisite to obtaining a pardon, which may relieve such a bar. Cal. Penal §§ 4852.01(a)-(d) and 4852.17. See also http://www.bpt.ca.gov/pardon_txt.html.

Public Assistance and Food Stamps

1. **Are people with drug-felony convictions dated after 1996 eligible to receive TANF benefits and food stamps?**

No, California adopted the federal drug felon ban. Cal. Wel. & Inst. §§ 11251.3 and 18901.7.

Public Housing

1. **Does the Housing Authority consider arrests that did not lead to conviction in its admission criteria?**

No, the Housing Authority of the City of Los Angeles (HACLA) does not consider arrests.

2. **Does the Housing Authority make individual determinations about an applicant's eligibility based upon the relevance of the criminal record?**

Yes, evidence of rehabilitation, such as the prospective resident's participation in, or willingness to participate in, counseling or another program will be considered if "unfavorable information" is revealed by HACLA's criminal history request. Unfavorable information suggests that the applicant poses a risk to children under age 18, and the aged, blind, and disabled.

3. **How long is the conviction bar(s)?**

While HACLA has access to convictions for all serious felonies, except those committed while a minor or more than 10 years ago, no bars exist. Cal. Penal Code §§ 1105.03(a)(1),(3),(4), and 1192.7(c)(1).

Voting

1. Does the state grant people with criminal records the right to vote?

Yes, people who have completed their sentences or who are on probation have the right to vote. However, people who are incarcerated or on parole following felony convictions are ineligible to vote. Cal. Const. Art. 2, § 4; Flood v. Riggs, 80 Cal.App.3d 138, 155 (1978).

The Legal Action Center 2004 Report
"What's the Law?"

Georgia

Driver's License Privileges

1. Does the state revoke or suspend the driver's licenses of people convicted of drug-related offenses?

The state suspends driver's licenses for drug-related offenses. Ga. Code Ann. § 40-5-75.

2. If so, what crime(s) result in suspension or revocation?

Driving under the influence and a range of drug-related offenses. Ga. Code Ann. § 40-5-75(a).

3. If so, what is the length of the suspension or revocation?

At least 180 days for first conviction, with longer suspensions for subsequent convictions occurring within five years. Ga. Code Ann. § 40-5-75(a).

4. Does the state offer restricted driver's licenses for purposes of employment, education, and/or medical care?

Yes, following a two-year waiting period an individual convicted for the third time may apply for a three-year driving permit for purposes of transportation to and from school, work, medical care, or addiction support groups. Ga. Code Ann. § 40-5-75(a).

Employment

1. Can employers ask job applicants about arrests not leading to conviction?

Yes.

2. Can employers consider arrests not leading to conviction?

Yes.

3. Does the state have standards prohibiting employment discrimination by public employers and occupational licensing agencies based on a conviction record?

No.

4. Does the state have standards prohibiting employment discrimination by private employers based on a conviction record?

No.

5. Does the state restrict people with criminal records from employment in the field of home health care?

No.

6. After an individual has been convicted, does the state offer any mechanism to demonstrate that an individual has been rehabilitated?

Restoration of civil and political rights (automatically granted to felony parolees upon discharge from supervision if no other sentence or pending charges; can apply if complete sentence or serve specified number of years on parole with satisfactory adjustment in society) and pardons. Ga. Code Ann. § 42-9-42 and Ga. Comp. R. & Regs. r. 475-3-.10(6). Neither restoration of rights nor a pardon automatically lifts occupational bars. State of Georgia, Board of Pardons and Paroles: Other forms of clemency, available at http://www.pap.state.ga.us/other_forms_clemency.htm (last accessed Nov. 20, 2002).

Public Assistance and Food Stamps

1. Are people with drug-felony convictions dated after 1996 eligible to receive TANF benefits and food stamps?

No, Georgia adopted the drug-felon ban. Ga. Code Ann. § 49-4-184.

Public Housing

1. Does the Housing Authority consider arrests that did not lead to conviction in its admission criteria?

Yes, the Atlanta Housing Authority considers violent and drug-related felony arrests.

2. Does the Housing Authority make individual determinations about an applicant's eligibility based upon the relevance of the criminal record?

Yes.

3. How long is the conviction bar(s)?

6 years bar for violent or drug-related convictions. Bar commences from the date of arrest.

Voting

1. Does the state grant people with criminal records the right to vote?

Persons convicted of a felony involving moral turpitude are disqualified from voting until completion of the sentence. Ga. Const. Art. 2, § 1; Ga. Code Ann. § 21-2-216.

Recidivism

Recidivism means that an ex-offender has been sent back to jail or prison. The individual might have re-offended or been sentenced to incarceration because of a technical violation. When ex-offenders engage in activities that break their parole or probation contracts, they can be sentenced to serve more time. These technical violations account for a significant portion of the recidivism rate. In Texas, for example, in fiscal year 2004 almost half of the 77,000 inmates entering prison were incarcerated because they violated their conditions of probation or parole, not because they committed a new crime (*Houston Chronicle* 2005, 10).

A district judge can revoke probation and send an ex-offender back to prison for merely being fifteen minutes late for a meeting. A legislative study found that many nonviolent offenders believe that serving prison time is easier than meeting all the rigid requirements of a probation or parole contract. There are monthly drug tests, supervisory fees, mandatory community service hours, and court-ordered attendance at regular substance-abuse treatment and anger-management sessions (*Houston Chronicle* 2005, 10).

States are unwittingly putting their resources into incarcerating parole and probation violators when non-penal, less costly alternatives are readily available. As John Whitmire, Texas state senator, observes, "The huge issue is revoking probationers." He continues, "I understand we have to be firm with probationers, but if they have not committed a new crime, I don't think they should be sent to prison. We have got to break this trend toward expanding our prison system when it's being led by nonviolent offenders" (*Houston Chronicle* 2005, 10).

Fred Steed has something to say about why recidivism rates are so high in the state of Georgia. After our telephone conversation about prison conditions, I asked him to comment on this issue.

You asked me about the recidivism rate. I think it will remain high because brothers are doing ten years or more and paroling out or maxing out with no educational background or skilled training. During Commissioner Wayne Gardner's era, Georgia lawmen and the "powers that be" made an across-the-board agreement to a "get tough on crime" policy. With this policy came more prison time, no educational programs, no skilled training, and to make it more humiliating, the State marked "State Prisoner" (in bold print) on everything including our underwear. While in prison, I witnessed many young brothers, mostly between the ages of 18 and 24, who could not read or write any better than a 4th grader. Not only did these young brothers not know that it is important to be literate, they did not seem to care—and the worst thing about the situation is nobody else seemed to care either. The whole "get tough on crime" policy paints a negative picture. It brought shame, disgrace, and embarrassment for brothers to wear "State Prisoner" over their backs, on their hats, etc. It was like we were the mark of a beast. It was very sad to see the State disgrace a lot of younger brothers and older men like that. Also during the "get tough on crime" era I watched in outrage as the State robbed education to finance prisons. Robbing education to finance prisons only points to a bleaker future for our children. Decaying schools lead to a decaying society. This is clearly symbolized by a rising prison population and a high recidivism rate. While incarcerated, I studied the system, so I understood what the "powers that be" were doing. I knew there was no chance for me to further my education or get skilled training, so I, along with another inmate, founded a program called "Speech Craft" and with thirty or

*more members in each cycle, we all taught one another. It
was one of the greatest and most uplifting experiences of my
life. We also spoke to alternative, private, and public schools.
Doing positive deeds such as these helped me to overcome the
negative stigma that was placed upon my back. Martin
Luther King Jr. once said, "The ultimate measure of a man is
not where he stands in times of comfort and convenience but
where he stands in times of challenge and controversy." My
faith in God, my sincere prayers, and my relationship with
God helped me to stand firm in challenge or controversy. My
eight-year prison term became my Yale and Harvard. I didn't
focus on the bars. I focused on the space between the bars.*

More than 650,000 individuals are released from state and federal
prisons annually. They return to the low-income, mostly urban communities they left. Even if the ex-offender gets a job, housing, and access to education, his future is still bleak if he has children, as Jessica
Pearson points out in a report titled "Child Support and Incarceration." Some 70 percent of those who are delinquent in their child-
support payments make less than $10,000 per year. In May of 2003,
the supreme court of Pennsylvania denied a petition by a recently released inmate who claimed he could not pay child support because
of his incarceration. While in prison he had a job that paid him four
cents per hour—$50 per month. This decision overturned long-
standing Pennsylvania case law that stated those incarcerated were not
obligated to pay child support.

Months after the Pennsylvania decision, Wisconsin took a similar
action. The state's supreme court ordered an inmate to pay $543 per
month to support his three children while serving the remainder of
a three-year sentence for a DUI and cocaine possession. The court
was unsympathetic to his plea that he made only $60 per month in
the prison. Over the course of his incarceration, the inmate's back
payments amounted to $25,000, not including interest (Pearson
2004, 2).

States have adopted three general approaches to dealing with inmates' responsibilities for child support payments. The "No Justification Approach" states there is no justification for an inmate's child
support payments to be eliminated or reduced during incarceration.

Twenty-one states have embraced this approach. Thirteen states, including the District of Columbia, have taken the "Complete Justification Approach," which states that incarceration is sufficient justification for the elimination or reduction of existing child support payments. Eleven states have implemented the "One Factor Approach," which states that incarceration is just one of many factors used to determine whether to reduce or eliminate child support payments (Pearson 2004, 2).

Although judicial discretion in child support cases has been reduced and often replaced by mathematical formulas used to calculate child-support payments, judges still have some autonomy. A judge who orders a recently released inmate to make up payments for the time spent in prison dooms the ex-offender. Likewise, the ex-offender is doomed if the judge orders unreasonable payments while the individual is adjusting to life in the free world. The ex-offender is in danger of violating the law at every turn (Pearson 2004, 1).

Langan and Levin (2002) found that of 272,111 prisoners released in fifteen states, 67.5 percent were rearrested for a serious misdemeanor or a felony within three years. This alarming recidivism rate is a threat to public safety. There are many victims resulting from the crimes of repeat offenders. Some 46.9 percent of free felons were convicted of a new crime and 25.4 percent were re-sentenced for a new crime. Moreover, 51.8 percent of free felons were serving time in prison for a technical violation of their probation or parole. With so much emphasis in political discourse focused on public safety, it is amazing that politicians fail to acknowledge the connection between public safety and recidivism. Elyse Clawson, executive director of the Crime and Justice Institute in Boston, is right when she says, "People tend to want to incarcerate [offenders] and not think about them, and then they consider it public safety, but if you don't do something while they're there, it's very short public safety" (Cramer 2004, 1).

As the Urban Institute states, everyone benefits when an ex-offender successfully reintegrates into society. It is a win-win scenario for politicians and for the public. With the Mentally Ill Offender Treatment and Crime Reduction Act of 2004, Congress appropriated $100 million to help communities prepare for the return of a record number of prisoners. Recent reentry initiatives have been supported in every state. The U.S. Departments of Justice, Labor, Health and Human Services, Housing and Urban Development, and Education have combined their budgets to support reentry initiatives, technical assistance, and the evaluation of reentry programs (Solomon et al. 2004, 11).

I have learned, as a student of public policy, that the market is inefficient at dealing with certain things in society. It cannot deal, for example, with issues such as public goods or social equity. If the market had been able to deal effectively with the issue of desegregation, government intervention would not have been necessary. It is the role of government, in the case of ex-offender reentry, to provide educational opportunities, job training, and job opportunities to inmates reentering society. The government should encourage big businesses to hire free felons, through tax incentives and other means. It is after all in the best interest of the government to reduce recidivism rates. And yet federal and state governments are the primary culprits in stigmatizing ex-convicts. They are explicitly prohibited from working in hundreds of federal and state jobs, for example.

The average cost of housing an inmate hovers around $25,000 per year. From a cost versus benefit perspective, current prison policies are irrational. It makes more sense for the government to invest in policies intended to prevent crime in the first place: preschool and K-12 education, recreational and after-school programs, job training, and substance-abuse treatment programs. An overwhelming majority of prison inmates are high-school dropouts and/or have some type of substance abuse problem. Lawmakers should consider the root causes of criminal activity when attempting to decrease its incidence and its impact on society.

The prison systems should adopt policies that prepare individuals to be self-sufficient once they are released from prison. Successful reentry programs take a holistic approach in dealing with ex-offenders. They confront important issues such as employment, family life, health, public safety, housing, and education. It should be the role of the government to provide opportunities that allow free felons to overcome formidable challenges in these and other areas in order to become self-sufficient.

References

Bureau of Justice Statistics. 2004. *Probation and Parole Statistics Summary Findings*. Washington, DC: U.S. Department of Justice. Accessed 30 March 2005 at http://www.ojp.usdoj.gov/bjs/.

Cramer, Maria. 2004. Release program hopes to keep prisoners from making return trip. *Boston Globe*, 25 July.

Georgia Board of Pardons and Paroles. 2002. *Criminal Justice Brief: Parolees Keep Working Despite Economic Downturn*. Number 72, 6 February.

Houston Chronicle. 2005. Clogging the system. 27 January.

Joyner, Tammy. 2001. They want to work: Sometimes the only thing standing between a job seeker and a job is the lack of a car or clothes or having a criminal record. *Atlanta Journal-Constitution*, 4 February.

Langan, P. and D. Levin. 2002. *Recidivism of Prisoners Released in 1994*. Bureau of Justice Statistics NJC 193427. Washington, DC: U.S. Department of Justice.

Legal Action Center. 2004. *After Prison: Roadblocks to Reentry. A Report on State Legal Barriers Facing People With Criminal Records*. April.

Mauer, Marc. 2004. Too many black men out of work. *New York Times*, 21 July.

National Urban League. 2004. *The State of Black America*. Washington, DC: National Urban League.

Pearson, Jennifer. 2004. *Child Support and Incarceration*. Center for Policy Research. July.

Solomon, Amy L., Michelle Waul, Asheley Van Ness, and Jeremy Travis. 2004. *Outside the Walls: A National Snapshot of Community-Based Prisoner Reentry Programs*. Urban Institute in collaboration with Outreach Extensions.

Steed, Frederick. 2004. Telephone interview regarding life as a free felon. 11 August.

Usborne, David. 2004. Seven million doing time as US prisons over-flow. *The Independent*, 27 July.

von Zielbauer, Paul. 2005. Study shows more job offers for ex-convicts who are white. *New York Times*, 17 June.

Chapter 5

Ignoble Laws

We are all Lynndie England because we know what's happening in our prisons and we don't care. Following the example of a leader who proudly sees no nuance, we tell ourselves the convenient lie that anyone who bears the label "criminal" or "terrorist" is irredeemable, subhuman psycho scum, and so whatever happens to them behind bars is justified, when the truth is millions of nonviolent Americans have been traumatized for life in prisons simply because they either did drugs or made a bad judgment, usually when they were young, stupid and drunk … In conclusion, if your response to this is "Not my problem," remember this: There are monsters and animals in our prisons, yes, but most didn't go in that way, but that's how they'll come out. (Maher 2004, B5)

In 2003, there were 715 inmates in the U.S. for every 100,000 residents. According to The Sentencing Project, this is the highest rate of incarceration in the world. By comparison, Russia—a nation whose incarceration rates once paralleled those of the U.S.—now has 584 inmates per 100,000 residents. Mexico has 169; Canada, 116; and England and Wales, 143 (Cass 2004, A7).

In 2003, the U.S. inmate population grew at its fastest rate in four years. The number of inmates increased by 3.9 percent in local jails, 1.8 percent in state prisons, and 7.1 percent in federal prisons. Racial and ethnic minorities made up 68 percent of the total number of inmates. An estimated 12 percent of the entire black male population in their 20s were incarcerated, as were 3.7 percent of Latino men, and 1.6 percent of white men in this age group (Cass 2004, A7). The Justice Department's Bureau of Justice Statistics attributes the alarming rise in the prison population to the "get tough on crime" policies of the 1980s and 90s. Laws directed at repeat offenders have restricted early-release policies and caused court backlogs, prison overcrowding, and fiscal nightmares.

Three Strikes Laws

Notwithstanding the death penalty, the three strikes law is the most discussed criminal justice policy in the U.S. These and other habitual offender laws now on the books in some form in almost half the states were born of the 1994 federal Violent Crime Control and Law Enforcement Act. Alabama and California are two of the states that have unduly harsh repeat offender laws.

Many nonviolent criminals are serving life sentences because of Alabama's Habitual Felony Offender Law. Samuel Thompson is one. He was arrested for his first burglary at the age of 18 and committed five nonviolent property crimes by the time he was 30. In 1983, the 51-year-old grandfather was charged with his third strike and sentenced to life in prison after he put a gun to a cashier's head while robbing an Ensley Chicken restaurant of $103. Ironically, two years after Thompson's robbery, the cashier he robbed shot a man in the face. She pleaded guilty to manslaughter and was given probation. Although Thompson never injured or killed anyone, he is serving a life sentence at the St. Clair prison. Thompson has been a model inmate, with only one disciplinary write-up. He has a reputation for being trustworthy, and the prison staff lets him run errands. Nevertheless, he has no chance of getting out of prison. Thompson says, "I feel like 20 years, to me, I feel like it's enough. But if it's not enough, if they want me to do 30 years, if I can live 10 more years, I'll live it." He continues, "All I'm asking for is a second chance in society to show that I can do right. You got to learn from your mistakes, and I done learned" (Crowder 2004[a], 12A).

Vietnam veteran Douglas Lamar Gray is another casualty of Alabama's tough repeat-offender law. Gray owned his own profit-making roofing business and had a wife and a child. As a teen, he had been locked up for a few months for burglary and committed two more robberies when he was in his early 20s. In 1989, when he was 49—and had not been arrested for 14 years—Gray bought $900 of marijuana after being lured into a motel by a police informant with a criminal record. After his purchase Gray drove away into a sea of police cars and was soon arrested. None of Gray's offenses were violent. No one was ever hurt. Nevertheless, Gray's offense of buying at least 2.2 pounds of marijuana constituted his third strike. He received a life sentence from the Morgan County district attorney and will die in prison. Gray's ex-wife commented on the injustice of his sentence when she said, "I think there's something wrong with the law when there's a child abuser and killers out here and he's locked up for the rest of his life for what he done." The man who served his nation fighting in Vietnam garnered no sympathy from the society he once fought to protect (Crowder 2004[b], 1).

California residents, moved by the kidnapping and brutal death of a young girl named Polly Klaas, approved that state's three strikes law in 1994. It was a bold policy intended to remove violent and serious offenders from society. According to the law, "If a defendant has two or more prior felony convictions that have been pled and proved, the term for the current felony conviction shall be an indeterminate term of life imprisonment." An offender who commits a third offense faces 25 years to life in prison if the first two offenses were serious felonies. In the same spirit, the sentences of second-strike felons are doubled and, under another law, first-strike violent felons must serve at least 85 percent of their sentences before they are eligible for parole.

These three strike laws are harsh in theory and in practice. In many instances, their application has proven to be seriously flawed, unjust, and unfair. California voters thought they were voting to put away repeat offenders who committed three violent or serious crimes. However, deeply embedded in this law is this provision: "The prosecuting attorney may move to dismiss or strike a prior felony conviction in the furtherance of justice." The discretion to strike previous felonies from a particular defendant's record rests solely with the district attorney.

What makes California's three strikes law the harshest in the nation is that—unlike the 24 other states with similar laws—it stipulates that any felony, not necessarily a serious one, can be considered a third strike. Throughout the state, nearly 60 percent of "third-strikers" are incarcerated for committing nonviolent crimes such as shoplifting, evading arrest, drug possession, and check fraud (*San Francisco Chronicle* 2004[b], E4).

The average annual cost of housing an inmate in California is $31,000. If this amount is multiplied by 25 years of prison time, the expense to the state of maintaining each third-striker is at least $775,000. Some 87,000 inmates have been affected by the longer sentences required by the law adding about $500 million a year to the state's corrections budget (Martin 2005, B4). California's Department of Corrections and Rehabilitation, the largest agency in the state, has an annual budget that is approaching more than $7 billion. Could this money be better spent? At the time the three strikes law passed, Stanford Law School criminal law scholar Robert Weisberg said three strikes "is a fiscal catastrophe and ludicrous as a matter of policy." He went on to state, "We already have a heavy set of repeat-offender laws, so the marginal, additional deterrent value is probably zilch, while the cost is unbelievable" (Moore 2004, B15; *Christian Science Monitor* 2004, 8). In 2004, the governor of California convened a blue-ribbon panel to examine why the state's prison system has spiraled out of control in costs, recidivism, and charges of abuse. Prison management now lacks both transparency and accountability.

According to the state's department of corrections, there are 235 inmates serving 25 years to life for car theft. There are more than 10,000 inmates incarcerated whose second and third strikes were for drug offenses (Martin 2004, A1).

While it is true that California's crime rate has been cut in half in the ten years since the three strikes law was implemented, the law's supporters cannot establish that reduced crime rates have resulted exclusively because of this law. In the 24 other states with similar laws, crime has decreased even more dramatically than in California—even though California's law is the most stringent (*Christian Science Monitor* 2004, 8).

After two decades of embracing punitive criminal justice policies, California residents are making a reluctant shift regarding offenders and ex-offenders. The state's voter-generated Proposition 66 sought to soften the state's three strikes law. Under Proposition 66, an individual's second and third strikes would have to be serious felonies. This was to be applied retroactively, which meant that some 4,000 to 7,000 inmates in California would be eligible to apply for re-sentencing. Throughout the campaign for Proposition 66, support for it hovered at 65 to 70 percent. However, only four weeks before the election, California's governor and crime-victim advocates launched a blistering $7 million television ad campaign against it. This campaign, aided by the governor's appearance on the *Tonight Show*, proved very effective. The governor maintained that if the proposition were approved, it would lead to the release of "26,000 dangerous criminals." In four weeks, the proposition lost public support and was defeated at the polls, 53 to 47 percent. Based on survey results, 1.5 million California voters, exposed to the barrage of anti-66 commercials, changed their minds in the last ten days of the campaign. Poll observers had never witnessed such a sharp turnaround (Walters 2004, A3).

Even when the public becomes more progressive and gives the signal for change, influential public officials want to hold on to the draconian policies of the past. It is sad to see people of influence disconnected from reality. It is equally sad to watch people operate without compassion or good judgment. Surprisingly—and most disappointingly—the courts are also culpable of acting with insensitivity.

The case of Native American Keith Carmony is just one of many that highlight the flaws in California's original three strikes law. Carmony, who battled alcoholism his entire life, spent time in prison for two serious offenses. After his release he was required to register as a sex offender, and he did. The law stipulates that a sex offender must re-register each year within five days of their birthday. Carmony, who originally registered three and a half weeks before his birthday, failed to re-register within five days. This technical violation was counted as Carmony's third strike, and he was sentenced to life in prison. The California Courts of Appeal overturned his life sentence, calling his crime "the most technical violation [of the sex offender law] we have seen." Nevertheless, in 2004 the California State Supreme Court overruled the appeal court and thereby affirmed the application of the three strikes law even when the third strike was a relatively minor crime. The court declared that the trial judge had acted entirely within the parameters of the law by giving Carmony a life sentence.

A few judges who voted to keep Carmony in prison for life later expressed reservations about their decision. Justice Carlos Moreno, for example, wrote, "it is difficult to escape the conclusion that the electorate that enacted the 'three strikes' law did not intend to impose a life sentence on someone whose last offense was a technical violation of the sex offender statute ... that posed no danger to the public" (*San Francisco Chronicle* 2004[a], B8).

If society cannot count on justices to exercise judicial review, who can it count on? One of the fundamental roles of the state and federal supreme courts is to judge whether laws passed by the citizenry or legislature are constitutional. Our three-tiered governance structure was designed to create checks and balances. It was also designed to prevent the tyranny of the majority. When lawmakers and society have acted in ways counter to the spirit of the Constitution, it is the role of the highest courts to put them back on the right course. Since the landmark 1803 case of *Marbury v. Madison*, this has been the Supreme Court's most important charge. In the context of the totalitarian-like three strikes laws, the highest courts have failed their roles as interpreters of the Constitution. They have failed our society. One clear example of this failure on the state level is the Carmony case. One clear example of this failure on the federal level is the 2003 U. S. Supreme Court decision, upholding 5-4 the legitimacy of three strikes laws. The Supreme Court ruled in two California cases that the state's three strikes law did not yield "grossly disproportionate" sentences that violate the Eighth Amendment of the U.S. Constitution.

Justice Anthony Kennedy, who, ironically, voted to uphold three-strikes laws, stated:

> It is a grave mistake to retain a policy just because a court finds it constitutional. Courts may conclude that the legislature is permitted to choose long sentences, but that does not mean long sentences are wise or just. Few misconceptions about government are more mischievous than the idea that a policy is sound simply because a court finds it permissible. A court decision does not excuse the political branches or the public from the responsibility for unjust laws. (Kennedy 2003)

In my political science courses, I ask my students whether they think the Supreme Court should reflect the will of the people or rise above it, if doing so is right. The overwhelming majority of my students believe the Supreme Court should rise up and do the right thing. It was the controversial rulings of the Warren Court that embraced civil rights and civil liberties in the 1950s and 60s and changed the course of this nation. If the Supreme Court does not consistently interpret the Constitution as a document that protects the rights of all citizens from haphazard and unfair treatment, then a serious problem exists in this society. Even those on the fringe should be shielded by the Constitution from draconian policies.

Drug Laws

The film *Traffic*—nominated for an Academy Award in 2000—gives us a grim, candid, and comprehensive look at drug trafficking and drug abuse. Directed by Steven Soderbergh and featuring stars such as Michael Douglas, Don Cheadle, Benicio Del Toro, and Catherine Zeta-Jones, *Traffic* shows how the so-called War on Drugs has failed. Billions of dollars have been spent in vain to prevent drug use and trafficking. Tens of thousands of people have been incarcerated because of their connection to illicit drugs. A high-school student in *Traffic* states, "For someone my age, it's a lot easier to get drugs than it is to get alcohol." The film also highlights the racial and class bias that exists in our society. Indeed, there are double standards. Affluent young adults often frequent the ghettos to buy their drugs. In fact, in the film the conservative drug czar's teenage daughter is a heroin addict. She is not sent to prison to serve a mandatory minimum sentence for possessing or using drugs. She is sent to a private treatment center for her addiction. Her illness is treated like a health problem rather than a crime.

African Americans make up approximately 14 percent of illegal drug users but 74 percent of those convicted for drug offenses. The War on Drugs did not meander through the hallowed halls and lawns of the Ivy League institutions in the U.S. Disproportionately harsh drug laws did not have an impact on my 1989 graduating class at Vanderbilt University. My very bright cohorts and I were matriculating during the height of the crack epidemic. Some states already had tough drug laws in place by 1989, while others were in the midst of formulating the most punitive drug laws in the nation's history. Nevertheless, my classmates who frequently smoked marijuana and used a variety of other drugs were completely unaffected by these laws. I don't recall any raids in the dormitories where drugs were being used. I don't remember any drug busts at fraternity or sorority houses. Some students regularly got their dope from the housing projects of Nashville. If they did not get their drugs directly from the 'hood, they were in regular contact with a middleman who did.

It always amazed me how there seemed to be no serious consequences for the wanton behavior of these affluent students. This phenomenon has come to be known as "white privilege." These young people were born on third base with all the privileges of the elite class. If the drug offending students at Ivy League schools and the children of politicians were being locked up for mandatory minimum sentences of 15 years to life starting tomorrow, what would be the response? Of course there would be reforms put in place the day *after* tomorrow. There would be no talk of how we have to work out the kinks in a complex situation and how the changes must be incremental and gradual. There would be no talk about what we will do with all the released offenders. There would be cohesion and consensus on the need for dramatic reforms.

Prosecutors are very reluctant to bring charges against a junior majoring in biology at Yale University, even though the student was found by authorities to be in possession of two ounces of narcotics. Why? The biology major is not seen as a threat to society. The young black man who lives in New Haven, however—five minutes from the prestigious institution—is seen as a threat to society, a menace. The perception is that the Yale student has the potential to contribute something positive to society. The young black man, however, is seen as lacking this capacity. Our current criminal justice policies suggest that he is assumed to be incorrigible and impossible to rehabilitate. What other conclusion can be drawn from the capricious application of mandatory minimum sentences of 15 years to life on people of different colors and classes?

Blacks have carried the burdens of their blackness since slavery, while whites have never suffered from their whiteness. Indeed, they have benefited, some more than others. They represent the elite. An African American writer highlights the significance of "privilege" in this commentary:

> I couldn't help but cringe the other night, watching a documentary on the Kennedy clan. Virtually all of the Kennedy kids had a drug problem, did heroin, did cocaine. Big time! You know where they went? To camp, to rehab. They glamorized it. But you know where our kids go: to jail! Now, those same Kennedy kids are running megamillion-dollar foundations, considering political office, even the presidency. If our kids get out of jail—and that's a big if, considering the mandatory drug-sentencing laws—they're condemned to a life of menial jobs, can't vote, and damn sure can't aspire to be president. (*Broward Times* 2004, 10)

One research study revealed there are almost five times as many white marijuana users as black users, four times as many white cocaine users as black users, and almost three times as many whites crack cocaine users as black users (Thompson 2003, A1). Despite these statistics, 74 percent of those incarcerated for drug offenses are black. How can these disparities be justified?

Senior U.S. District Court Judge Clyde S. Cahill died in 2004. A pioneer in the legal profession, he was the first black federal judge in St. Louis. Cahill spent his illustrious career as an advocate for the downtrodden, vulnerable, and defenseless. During his judgeship he made many scathing comments about the U.S. criminal justice system. His position, experience, and race gave him unique insights into the system's intricate dynamics. He is remembered for declaring the drug sentences handed out in crack cocaine cases to be unconstitutional because blacks were disproportionately targeted. They did not make up the majority of crack cocaine users. He also stated that the drug sentencing laws amounted to "unconscious racism by Congress and prosecutors" (*St. Louis Post-Dispatch* 2004, C8). Although his ruling in the drug sentencing case was overturned by the 8th Circuit Court of Appeals, Cahill's perspective should not be dismissed.

There is a well-known disparity in the sentences of those caught with crack cocaine and those caught with powder cocaine. In the mid-1980s Congress made a law stating that a person caught possessing five grams of crack cocaine (two rocks) would serve five years in jail, even if it was a first-time offense. In order for someone to get the equivalent sentence for powder cocaine, they would have to possess 500 grams. In other words, it would require 100 times more powder cocaine than crack cocaine to get the same five-year sentence. Why? Because the perception is that crack cocaine is the street drug of minorities and powder cocaine is the drug of the affluent. Indeed, powder cocaine has been the preferred drug of some lawmakers themselves and of their privileged children. At the time the tough crack cocaine drug law was passed, the theory was that crack cocaine was more addictive and caused more lawlessness. This has been proven to be untrue. But the racially motivated sentencing policy destroyed the lives of many minorities and their families. The U.S. Sentencing Commission has urged Congress to amend this glaringly biased policy, but Congress has not budged for the inexcusable fear of being seen as soft on drugs (Reese 2004; *International Herald Tribune* 2005).

The War on Drugs has focused intensely on urban communities with large minority populations. Policies that target minorities, the poor, and the powerless have always been attractive to lawmakers. This population is the most vulnerable and the easiest to exploit. Regardless of the toll on individuals, their families, and communities, lawmakers have enacted policies that reflect a legacy of hubris, insensitivity, and racial bias. The politicians who enact these policies consider themselves more progressive and culturally sensitive than their predecessors. They seem unaware that their policies have had a more debilitating affect on black men than any of the policies of the segregation era.

Although they are considered to be the most noble of American institutions, the courts—particularly the highest courts—have also failed minority communities. They have teamed with politicians to play the race game with matching fervor, insensitivity, and callousness. In 2002, for example, the Michigan Campaign for New Drug Policies (MCNDP) petitioned for first time drug offenders to be offered treatment instead of jail sentences. Although this group gathered 454,584 signatures—enough for their measure to be placed on the November ballot—the Michigan Supreme Court refused to give the drug-law reformers a slot on the ballot. The court upheld an earlier appeals court decision stating that MCNDP failed to show clearly a legal right to certification by the state board of canvassers. The board of canvassers did not support the MCNDP because they said the section of the group's drug reform initiative that would amend the state constitution was numbered incorrectly (Thompson 2003, A1).

What Martin Luther King Jr. had to say about the sociopolitical environment in 1963 also applies today.

> Even today there still exists in the South—and in certain areas of the North—the license that our society allows to unjust officials who implement their authority in the name of justice to practice injustice against minorities. Where, in the days of slavery social license and custom placed the unbridled power of the whip in the hands of overseers and masters, today—especially in the southern half of the nation—armies of officials are clothed in uniform, invested with authority, armed with the instruments of violence and death and conditioned to believe they can intimidate, maim or kill Negroes with the same recklessness that once motivated the slaveowner. (King 1964, 15)

Deborah Peterson Small, public policy director of the Drug Alliance in Washington, DC, makes a poignant comparison between slavery and today's criminal justice system:

> You can say, metaphorically, that the criminal justice system in America today is like a pipeline, like a slave ship transporting human cargo, primarily Black cargo, along interstate triangular trade-routes, from black and brown communities, through the middle passage of police precincts, holding pens, detention centers and court rooms to upstate or rural jails—and then back to communities as un-rehabilitated felons, and then back to jail, in a vicious cycle. (Thompson 2003, A1)

The models for the tough drug laws passed by many states in the 1980s and 1990s are the infamous Rockefeller laws. Enacted by New York Governor Nelson Rockefeller in 1973, these laws exemplify the most egregious human rights violations in the U.S. They are clear examples of the relevance of King's commentary on today's environment and Small's bondage metaphor. Governor Rockefeller called his drug laws the "toughest anti-drug program in the nation" (Baker 2004, A1). The minimum sentence for the sale of one ounce of narcotics or the possession of two ounces was 15 years to life. These laws also increased the penalties for those caught with smaller amounts of narcotics. Their purpose was to combat the upswing in drug activity in the state of New York. However, they have failed miserably. Of the 16,564 drug offenders imprisoned in New York in 2004, fewer than 3 percent—481 people—were incarcerated for the most serious drug offenses, called A-1 felonies. This number is lower than the number of serious drug offenders incarcerated in 1995, which was 724. What do these statistics mean? They mean that New York lawmakers have been playing insensitive political games. If only 3 percent of those incarcerated are serious drug offenders, these lawmakers are guilty of playing politics at the expense of thousands of individuals. They are guilty of sabotaging lives and adversely impacting families. Where is the sympathy? Where is the empathy? Where is the logic and rationality in locking up nonviolent minor drug offenders for 15 years to life? Many of those locked up are drug addicts. Alcoholics get sent to Alcoholics Anonymous for their addiction. Shouldn't drug addicts be sent to drug rehabilitation programs?

Politicians, ostensibly insightful guardians of the common good, have adopted inflexible and repressive drug policies. The cases of Elaine Bartlett and Anthony Papa are telling. Bartlett was arrested in Albany, New York, in 1983 for selling four ounces of cocaine. She was sentenced to 20 years to life for this first-time offense. In 1984, Papa served 12 years in prison for making a delivery of four and a half ounces of cocaine, worth $500 (Baker 2004). The case of Martha Weatherspoon also highlights the insensitivity of the Rockefeller laws. In 1989, at the age of 60, Weatherspoon entered Bedford Hills Correctional Facility. She had been sentenced to 20 years to life for selling eight ounces of cocaine to an undercover police officer. She was released 15 years later, when she was 75. If she had not been paroled—given time off for good behavior—she might have died in prison. Did Weatherspoon's punishment fit her crime? Compare Martha Weatherspoon's case to that of John Jamelske, one of Syracuse's most notorious criminals. Although he was found guilty of raping, kidnapping, and torturing five women, he was given a sentence of 18 years to life (Kirst 2004, A1; *Post-Standard* 2004, A8).

Lawmakers fail to take into account the devastating impact that incarceration has on the offender's family. In many cases, these harsh laws are counterproductive because of their negative ripple effect. What happens to the children of those given long-term sentences? Does it benefit society to have them grow up without a mother or father? One of Martha Weatherspoon's 35 grandchildren makes the point, "She was the backbone of our family [and] when she went away, everything kind of fell apart" (Kirst 2004, A1). Lawmakers need to realize that when they sentence someone to 15 years to life for a minor offense, they might be stealing someone else's role model.

Recently there has been a shift in thinking regarding drug users. New York politicians are finally becoming aware of the consequences of the unjust Rockefeller laws. Many in the New York legislature have embraced reforms. New York prosecutors have been directing defendants to drug rehabilitation programs. Because prosecutors have been the most callous players in this hard-edged game, their willingness to soften their stance offers real hope for change. The Republican governor states, "We have enacted some reforms over the course of the years and we have lessened the harshness of the pre-existing Rockefeller drug laws. But having said that, I still believe there is room for significant additional reform" (Baker 2004, A1).

While many politicians now agree that the drug laws are overly harsh and rigid, there is disagreement about how to make wrong policies right: how to ease sentences, how those already serving time will be impacted, and how much discretion should be given to judges to bypass the mandatory minimum sentencing laws (Baker 2004, A1). The need for such dramatic reforms suggests that politicians had it terribly wrong thirty years ago. It should not have taken this long to determine that these policies were unduly harsh and unjust.

In 2000, 61 percent of California voters approved Proposition 36, which mandated substance abuse treatment in lieu of incarceration for first or second time, nonviolent offenders convicted of simple drug possession. These offenders are referred to a Proposition 36 courtroom, where prosecutors, public defenders, probation officials, and treatment providers make decisions about treatment alternatives. This long overdue proposition makes sense. It allocates $120 million over more than five years to pay for drug treatment programs. In Ventura County, more than 4,000 drug offenders have received drug treatment instead of jail time; and to date, 280 have successfully completed the drug-abuse treatment program. Relapse is common with drug users because many in this population also suffer from alcoholism and/or mental illness. Overall, however, officials estimate that 40 percent of the participants in court-ordered treatment programs can be expected to overcome their addiction. The drug and alcohol administrators and others running the programs say that rehabilitation is working (Saillant 2003, B4). Even if fewer than half of all drug offenders recover, the Proposition 36 approach is still a more compassionate alternative that makes the most cost-effective use of taxpayers' money. Because the cost of treatment is so much less than the cost of incarceration, the projected savings as a result of Proposition 36 are estimated at $1.5 billion over five years, according to the Drug Policy Alliance (www.prop36.org).

In 2004, Alaska's Supreme Court upheld a state law that allows individuals to possess four ounces of marijuana in their homes for personal use. Voters in several states have approved the use of marijuana for medicinal purposes. It is amazing in the U.S. federalist system of governance that some states condone marijuana use while others punish and criminalize individuals for the same behavior.

Bill Piper (2005, B7), director of national affairs for the Drug Policy Alliance, offers thoughtful, coherent suggestions for a more rational U.S. drug policy:

- Reprioritizing resources toward high-level traffickers, violent criminals, and terrorists. Too many federal resources are wasted on low-level drug offenses that already are illegal under state law.

- Diverting nonviolent offenders to drug treatment instead of prison. Treatment is cheaper and more effective at reducing recidivism.

- Reforming harsh drug laws that punish nonviolent drug offenders more severely than rapists and murderers. Congress should eliminate mandatory minimum sentences for nonviolent drug offenses and direct the U.S. Sentencing Commission to develop appropriate sentences.

- Eliminating the 100-to-1 sentencing disparity between crack and powder cocaine offenses. This should be done by lowering the draconian crack penalties to equal those for powder cocaine rather than increasing penalties for powder offenses.

- Fixing drug conspiracy laws so offenders are punished only for the crimes they commit, not the crimes of people they associate with. In particular, Congress should ensure that abused or misguided women are not punished for the offenses of their husbands and boyfriends.

- Preventing people from being sent to prison because of unproven accusations. Congress should require corroborating evidence in all drug cases to prevent people from being convicted solely on the word of one person (who might be an informant who is paid for each person convicted or a drug offender getting a reduced sentence for testifying, for example).

- Repealing federal bans that deny student loans, welfare, and other benefits to former offenders. Congress should encourage—not prevent—drug offenders getting their lives back together.

Mandatory Minimum Sentencing

New Jersey imposes harsh mandatory minimum sentences for drug offenses. Perhaps not coincidentally, the state also has the nation's highest percentage of people of all races incarcerated for drug-related crimes. After years of witnessing the state's correctional institutions sink deeper into crisis, a Commission to Review Criminal Sentencing was created by the New Jersey legislature. This fifteen-member commission was created to explore alternatives to mandatory minimum sentencing and address racial disparities in the state's criminal justice system. An overwhelming 81 percent of New Jersey's prison population is African American or Latino. The task of reforming the state's system is formidable. Its 700-page criminal code has not been changed in 26 years (Aaron 2004, L11).

Eric E. Sterling, President of the Criminal Justice Policy Foundation, wrote an editorial in the *Washington Post* entitled "Outrageous Drug Sentencing." In his essay he states, "In 1986 I helped the House Judiciary Committee write laws intended to send similar messages when Congress passed long, mandatory minimum drug sentences. That was a terrible mistake." Sterling writes that conservative Supreme Court Justice Anthony Kennedy shares his sentiments. In 2003, Kennedy told the American Bar Association, "In too many cases, mandatory minimum sentences are unwise and unjust." He also stated, "Our resources are misspent, our punishments too severe, our sentences too long." Kennedy continues, "Ladies and gentleman, I submit to you that a 20-year old does not know how long ten or fifteen years is. One day in prison is longer than almost any day you and I have had to endure." He challenged the nation's lawyers to exercise their social responsibility wisely—emphasizing to them that their duties did not end with trials and appeals (*Washington Post* 2004, B06; *Salt Lake Tribune* 2004, A10).

The American Bar Association, disturbed at the injustice resulting from mandatory minimums, appointed a commission to examine punishment, incarceration, and sentencing. The commission has made a series of substantive recommendations, including its primary conclusion that mandatory minimum sentencing laws should be repealed.

A blunt commentary in the *Salt Lake Tribune* focuses on the impact that mandatory minimums have had on nonviolent offenders and the mentally ill: "Incarcerating nonviolent people who are mentally ill or are substance abusers is flat out stupid and inhumane. They can be treated for a fraction of the cost of imprisonment while improving the chance that they will not offend again. Locking them up without treatment does nothing to improve public safety, and it punishes both the taxpayers and the offenders unjustly" (2004, A10).

Tom Dillard, veteran defense attorney in Knoxville, Tennessee, states that mandatory minimums "want to impress the fear factor to the public, [making] people think crime is rampant and we're going to have to barricade ourselves in our houses." He continues, "Under mandatory minimums, you may get some of the people you're aiming at, but it's like a shotgun approach. You're going to hit people you didn't intend to" (Satterfield 2004, B1).

Erik Luna, a professor at the University of Utah College of Law, sees the multiple flaws in federal sentencing guidelines. "First, the sentences are promulgated not by Congress but by a bureaucratic entity, the U.S. Sentencing Commission. And they rest on the notion that people thousands of miles away who have not seen a defendant or heard the facts know more about an appropriate sentence than the judge who has heard all the facts and looked him in the face" (*Orange County Register* 2004, 1).

John S. Martin Jr., a federal judge for thirteen years, retired from his position partially because of his frustration with the overly harsh and rigid federal sentencing guidelines. Martin believes that he has given proportionate sentences to many defendants. However, there were times, he maintains, that his desire to make the punishment fit the crime conflicted with the law. In these times of conflict, the law always prevailed. Martin recalls being particularly troubled by sentencing a man to five years of prison time for selling a very small amount of crack cocaine. He says of the defendant, "He had turned his life around and was gainfully employed" (Manson 2004, B2).

In 2004, the U.S. Supreme Court ruled in a 5-4 decision that Washington State's sentencing guidelines were unconstitutional. This decision in *Blakely v. Washington* sparked intense discussion about the legitimacy of all federal sentencing guidelines. In this case, the defendant received a four-year sentence for abducting his wife at knifepoint. Without consulting the jury, the judge added on three extra years for "deliberate cruelty." The Supreme Court ruled that this decision violated the defendant's constitutional right to a trial by jury.

The Bush administration, which supports mandatory minimums, requested that the Supreme Court review two drug cases that could determine the constitutionality of federal guidelines and affect 64,000 cases per year. In a decision that surprised many, the Court ruled in the 2005 cases of *U.S. v. Booker* and *U.S. v. Fanfan* that the federal sentencing guidelines are advisory and that judges do not have to follow them in every case. This ruling only affects federal sentencing guidelines, which are established by the U.S. Sentencing Commission (Piper 2005, B7).

Federal sentencing guidelines were enacted during the 1980s get-tough-on-crime era. They were wide ranging. From tax evasion to drug trafficking, laws were established to ensure consistent, uniform sentencing from state to state. In theory this policy is equitable and fair. However, in practice it is terribly flawed, because every case is different. The backgrounds, motivations, and circumstances of each crime are unique. Rigid, inflexible, one-size-fits-all laws cannot appropriately deal with the many variations of human behavior. On the other hand, judicial discretion has also resulted in flagrantly biased decisions over the years. The strength of uniform laws—including mandatory minimums—is that they take discretion away from potentially biased judges. The irony is that the strength of these laws also constitutes their fundamental weakness. When judges have more discretion, they have consistently meted out harsher punishments to African Americans. Mandatory minimum sentences have also had a disproportionately negative impact on the black population. Historically, blacks find themselves in these sorts of catch-22s.

Trying Teens as Adults

In the 2005 case of *Roper v. Simmons*, the U.S. Supreme Court banned capital punishment for juvenile offenders. Supreme Court Justice Anthony Kennedy wrote, "It would be misguided to equate the failings of a minor with those of an adult." The Court's decision affected the twenty states that allowed juries to sentence 16- and 17-year-olds to death. This ruling ended the dubious distinction of the United States as the only nation in the world to condone the execution of people who commit crimes when they are under the age of 18 (Lane 2005, A17). The fact that the Court's decision was 5-4 in this case was disappointing, however. Such a close decision means that four individual justices in the noblest institution in the land are out of step with the rest of the world. It is more disappointing that these individuals reflect the mindset of many citizens and lawmakers throughout the U.S.

The nation's first juvenile court opened in Chicago in 1899. The philosophy of this court was to make a distinction between offenses committed by children and offenses committed by adults. Traditionally, juveniles have been treated differently in the criminal justice system. It has been more lenient toward youth who commit crimes. In the past fifteen years, however, this approach has changed. Youth who perpetrate violent crimes are now being prosecuted as adults and sentenced to time in adult prison facilities. They are also being sentenced to mandatory adult sentences, such as life in prison without the possibility of parole. In an effort to punish crime by any means, the U.S. justice system has gone against its own foundations and against the philosophy embraced by other Western nations and indeed, the entire international community. The most troubling element of this cynical trend is its racist disparities. Young blacks are disproportionately sentenced as adults.

Western nations historically have adopted different perspectives regarding juvenile justice. For instance, England's juvenile courts, as in many states in the U.S., resemble adult courts. Their primary objective is to punish youthful offenders. In Scandinavian countries, youth under the age of 15 are, by law, incapable of committing crimes. Social welfare agencies deal with serious juvenile misconduct. Although adult courts in Sweden process those between the ages of 15 and 17, these young offenders cannot be sent to prison. In Scotland, juvenile crime is also handled by the social welfare system. Canada and Germany have adopted clear and rigid distinctions between juvenile and adult offenders. In New Zealand, all youthful offender cases are dealt with by conference, embracing a restorative judicial philosophy. The single shared feature of juvenile justice systems in Western countries is that young offenders should be treated differently than adults. Indeed, many international conventions have outlined protections for children. The European Convention for the Protection of Human Rights and Fundamental Liberties and the United Nations Convention on the Rights of the Child are two notable examples. The U.S. is not bound by the UN Convention because it is not a signatory of the pact (Tonry and Doob 2004).

Florida tries more children as adults than any other state in the U.S. In fact, Florida is the home of one of the most publicized and controversial cases in the country. In 1999, 12-year-old Lionel Tate killed his six-year-old playmate, Tiffany Eunick. Tate said he was imitating wrestling moves that he saw on television. In January 2001,

Tate entered a maximum-security juvenile prison after he was convicted of first-degree murder and given the mandatory adult sentence of life in prison without the possibility of parole. He was the youngest person in U.S. history to receive such a sentence. As Andrew Carter, a professor at Seattle University Law School, states, "Tate certainly deserved a stiff punishment but even his prosecutors struggled to identify some legitimate justification for putting a sixth-grade boy behind bars and throwing away the key. Rehabilitation? Deterrence? Retribution? Incapacitation? None of the traditional penological rationales seemed to justify so enduring a sentence" (2004, B9).

Tate's mother, and supporters who thought his punishment was overly harsh, won the sympathy of the United Nations and Pope John Paul II. This international scrutiny exposed the insensitivity of the Florida law that treats young people as adults and eventually led to the sentence being overturned by a Florida appeals court. The appeal was based on the fact that Tate had no pre-trial evaluation regarding his capacity to understand the complexities of the legal proceedings in his case. Tate's sentence was reduced to time served (Chandler 2004, 5). Florida's draconian law of sentencing children as adults remains unchanged, however. Every year since Tate was sentenced, a bill has been introduced into the Florida legislature to prohibit trying children as adults. Each time, the bill has failed to get the required number of votes to pass (Carter 2004, B9).

Florida State Senator Steve Geller has been a major proponent of changing Florida's sentencing laws. He wants children younger than 15 to be eligible for parole but only after they serve eight years of a life sentence. This would apply only to juvenile offenders with no prior criminal record who have been convicted as adults for murder. Eight years of incarceration is no slap on the wrist. His proposal strikes a balance between punishment and hope. Geller says, "Children are not simply short adults. They are different from adults and should be treated accordingly. We must impose punishments that fit the crime, but at the same time, provide opportunities for rehabilitation" (Hollis 2004, B5).

Florida State Senator Victor Crist, a Republican from Tampa, has led the opposition to changing the sentencing laws. He says the children who are serving life sentences for murder are not innocent people who accidentally killed someone. "These are young people who from the very beginning have that bad, evil, mean, violent seed in them," he maintains. "To let them out regardless of whether it's 5 years, 10 years, 30 years ... would be a crime itself. The law was written to be clear. If you take a person's life, you're going to serve a life sentence"(Hollis 2004, B5). Crist's perspective is devoid of sensitivity. He does not differentiate a 10-year-old from a 30-year-old. He reflects the sentiment of the staunchest tough-on-crime politicians. It is politicians such as Crist who have betrayed the spirit of our foundational democratic philosophy.

Why would Florida and other states choose to sentence teens as adults? The simple answer to this question addresses all the ignoble laws discussed in this chapter. Politicians want to be tough on crime, and their passion for this extends to 12-year-old children. They have chosen to exercise their bravado on minority populations. Poor black youth are the most despised and underrepresented group in America, and they have consistently been the primary target of politicians. As Carter candidly states,

> Studies strongly suggest that locking up a few 12-year-olds forever will have no impact on juvenile crime rates. But that is probably beside the point. In Florida, like elsewhere, the goal is votes, and empty crime-policy gestures often do the trick. For politicians, there really isn't a downside to building "tough-on-crime" credentials by voting for ever harsher sentences for adolescent offenders. Children who serve the mandatory adult sentences—usually poor African American boys—don't have a lobby. Their families and communities are not electoral considerations. (2004, B9)

In 1994, the Georgia State Senate passed Senate Bill 440, which allows the judicial system to try teens as adults. Since the bill's implementation, 600 juveniles have been sentenced as adults. Nearly 83 percent were black.

**Georgia: Juveniles admitted to adult prisons with sentences
of at least 10 years without possibility of parole**

Year	Black (429)	White (89)
1994	1	0
1995	18	4
1996	61	4
1997	49	13
1998	68	12
1999	57	11
2000	48	10
2001	44	12
2002	32	13
2003	48	7

*Note: Originally judges could impose a lighter sentence if the juvenile was a
first offender. In 1998, the legislature eliminated that option.
Source: Ezzard 2004, F4.

These statistics represent a national trend. A study by the Wash-
ington-based Pretrial Services Resource Center showed that minority
youth comprise 80 percent of the juveniles tried in adult courts in the
eighteen largest urban areas in the U.S. (Ezzard 2004, F4).

In 2000, 62 percent of California voters approved Proposition 21,
which made it easier to prosecute juveniles as adults. The proposition
allows filing a case directly in adult court for those 14 years and older
who have been charged with certain crimes. By approving this proposition, voters stated that children who have only been in the world for
168 months have the maturity to consistently make rational decisions.
In adult prisons, teens are victimized and traumatized. Research studies have shown that youth offenders who are integrated with adults
in prison are five times more likely to report being raped and eight
times more likely to attempt suicide (Daniels 2004, B2). The National
Commission on Correctional Health Care declared the placement of
adolescents in adult prisons to be "detrimental to the health and developmental well-being of youth." According to the Commission,
"Adolescents are at an increased risk for developing depressive symp-

toms and anxiety symptoms." They are also prone to "self-mutilating behavior, suicide attempts, psychotic symptoms and aggressive behaviors toward others" (Warren 2003, B1). Trying teens as adults is saying that there is no hope for rehabilitation, that there is no chance to be saved or redeemed.

In California's Alameda County, Superior Court judge Trina Thompson Stanley does not embrace the mean spirit of Proposition 21. Politicians should learn from this African American judge who presides over the juvenile division of one of the most challenging courts in northern California. Stanley, who grew up in the Lower Bottoms of West Oakland, sentences her youth offenders to rigorous reading assignments and essays. It is her goal to inspire self-discovery and discipline by assigning various intellectual exercises. Not wanting to label or sentence first-time offenders to personal or institutional failure, she challenges these youth in alternative ways. Stanley—who also serves as the chair of the Educational Task Force for the juvenile court, charged with overseeing the education of state-raised children—comments, "Most essay and book-related assignments are reserved for first-time offenders and provide me with a road map for their needs and an insight to what's important to them." As writer Daphne Muse observes, "Oftentimes, she slams her gavel down with one hand and extends a book with the other. Judge Stanley introduces books to these young people as a gift of opportunity, not a sanction or sentence." Muse goes on, "One of her juvenile offenders may well re-enter her courtroom as a lawyer, judge or Nobel Laureate coming to give thanks for getting 'booked'" (Muse 2004, 18).

Critics of Stanley's approach would surely say her strategy is overly soft, naïve, and counterproductive, not acknowledging the fact that two decades of hyper-punitive criminal justice policies have been unduly harsh, naïve, and counterproductive. Stanley's approach to handling first-time juvenile offenders revolves around rehabilitation, compassion, and hope. Why not try hope, since despair has failed us so miserably?

References

Aaron, Lawrence. 2004. Changing the faces of the criminal justice system. *The Record* (Bergen County, NJ), 16 July.

Baker, Al. 2004. Time eases tough drug laws, but fight goes on. *New York Times*, 16 April.

Broward Times. 2004. Off the vine: Whoa! Blacks aren't doing well! 58, no. 10 (2 April).

Carter, Andrew. 2004. Mandatory sentences? Not for kids. *Seattle Post-Intelligencer*, 6 April.

Cass, Connie. 2004. Prison populations rise. Associated Press, 30 May.

Chandler, K. 2004. Lionel Tate savors sweet taste of freedom after three years behind bars. *Westside Gazette* (Ft. Lauderdale, FL), 11 February.

Christian Science Monitor. 2004. Adjusting "three strikes" law. 8 June.

Crowder, Carla. 2004[a]. Thief gets life but killer freed under state law. *The Birmingham News* (Birmingham, AL), 28 March.

Crowder, Carla. 2004[b]. Marijuana conviction seals life behind bars for Vietnam veteran. *The Birmingham News* (Birmingham, AL), 28 March.

Daniels, Cynthia. 2004. On the law; Juvenile justice groups oppose gang prevention bill. *Los Angeles Times*, 25 June.

Ezzard, Martha. 2004. Throwing away the key: Race and sentencing. *Atlanta Journal-Constitution*, 28 March.

Hollis, Mark. 2004. Panel opposes sentencing revisions. *South Florida Sun-Sentinel*, 1 April.

International Herald Tribune. 2005. Drug sentencing in America. 3 June.

Kennedy, Anthony. 2003. Annual American Bar Association speech, 9 August. Accessed 20 March 2005 at http://www.humanrightsfirst. org/us_law/inthecourts/ABA_2003_Meeting_Justice_Kennedy.pdf.

King, Martin Luther, Jr. 1964. *Why We Can't Wait*. New York: Signet Classics.

Kirst, Sean. 2004. Drug law debate comes home. *Post-Standard* (Syracuse, NY), 20 August.

Lane, Charles. 2005. Kennedy reversal swings Court against juvenile death penalty. *Washington Post*, 7 March.

Maher, Bill. 2004. Prisons make monsters of jailers and inmates. *Seattle Post-Intelligencer*, 14 August.

Manson, Pamela. 2004. Required sentence doesn't fit crime, group says. *Salt Lake Tribune*, 9 August.

Martin, Mark 2004. "3 strikes" faces test of scope on Nov. 2/Prop. 66 addresses debate, is the law effective or cruel? *San Francisco Chronicle*, 12 October.

Martin, Mark 2005. Bulk of "3 strikes" crimes nonviolent, study finds. *San Francisco Chronicle*, 21 October.

Moore, Konrad R. 2004. Cost should be a factor in prison sentence. *Los Angeles Times*, 19 May.

Muse, Daphne. 2003. Book'em! *Black Issues Book Review* 5, no. 5.

Orange County Register. 2004. Sentenced to chaos? 9 August.

Piper, Bill. 2005. Court offers chance for sentence reform. *Seattle Post-Intelligencer*, 8 February.

Post-Standard. 2004. Rocky Rockefeller laws: Lawmakers must find the will to fix archaic statutes. (Syracuse, NY), 30 August.

Reese, Renford. 2004. *American Paradox: Young Black Men*. Durham, NC: Carolina Academic Press.

Saillant, Catherine. 2003. Success of addicts doing treatment, not time. *Los Angeles Times*, 10 November.

Salt Lake Tribune. 2004. Don't throw keys away. 7 August.

San Francisco Chronicle. 2004[a]. Slamming the prison door. 14 July.

San Francisco Chronicle. 2004[b]. Vagaries of our "three strikes" law. 22 August.

Satterfield, Jamie. 2004. DOJ responds to minimum sentence dissenters," *New Sentinel* (Knoxville, TN), 18 August.

St. Louis Post-Dispatch. 2004. Justice for all. 20 August.

Thompson, Bankole. 2003. Reformers challenge preaches: Protect people, stop drug war. *Michigan Citizen* (Highland Park, MI) XXV, no. 46.

Tonry, Michael, and Anthony Doob. 2004. *Youth Crime and Youth Justice: Comparative and Cross-National Perspectives* 31. Chicago: University of Chicago Press.

Walters, Dan. 2004. Voter turnaround on Proposition 66 was a dramatic campaign event. *Sacramento Bee*, 16 November.

Warren, Jenifer. 2003. Inmate, 17, hanged self, officials say. *Los Angeles Times*, 3 July.

Washington Post. 2004. Outrageous drug sentencing. 18 July.

www.prop36.org. California Proposition 36: The Substance Abuse and Crime Prevention Act of 2000. Sacramento, CA: Drug Policy Alliance.

Chapter 6

Assault on Human Rights

We will encourage reform in other governments by making
clear that success in our relations will require the decent
treatment of their own people. America's belief in human
dignity will guide our policies. Yet, rights must be more than
the grudging concessions of dictators; they are secured by
free dissent and the participation of the governed. In the long
run, there is no justice without freedom, and there can be no
human rights without human liberty. (President George W.
Bush, 2005 Inaugural Address)

In 2005, a report by Amnesty International condemned the U.S.
government for its treatment of suspected terrorists held at Guantanamo Bay, Cuba. The report compared Guantanamo to the Soviet
gulags, where dissidents were sent without trial, and accused the U.S.
of turning its back on its responsibility to set standards for the protection of human rights around the world. President Bush called the
allegations of prisoner mistreatment "absurd" and dismissed them as
coming from "people who hate America." Vice President Dick Cheney
said he was "offended" by the report, stating, "I frankly just don't take
[Amnesty International] seriously." U.S. Defense Secretary Donald
Rumsfeld called the allegations "reprehensible" and said the organization's report "cannot be excused" (Jones 2005, 10).

In response to the President's statement about the allegations being
absurd, William Schulz, the executive director of Amnesty International, USA, stated, "What is 'absurd' is President Bush's attempt to
deny the deliberate policies of his administration, which has detained
individuals without charge or trial in prisons at Guantanamo Bay,
Bagram Air Base, and other locations. What is 'absurd' and indeed

outrageous is the Bush administration's failure to undertake a full independent investigation" (Knowlton 2005, 4). In the *Los Angeles Times*, Robert Scheer pointed out, "What is reprehensible is letting dogs attack naked prisoners, shipping others out to be tortured by totalitarian regimes and covering up the deaths of prisoners during interrogations" (2005, B13).

There are governments around the world that enthusiastically embrace injustice and human rights violations. A safely anonymous government official from the Sudan will likely admit that his government is flawed and corrupt. Freed from persecution for making truthful comments, government officials from China, Nigeria, Libya, Saudi Arabia, and Russia would likely acknowledge the flaws of their system of governance. U.S. officials, however, have touted their system of justice to be an exemplary model for the world. They seek to export the country's flawless morality and to consistently condemn others for human rights violations. However, there are human rights violations taking place throughout America's prisons.

Angola

The Louisiana State Penitentiary in Angola is the largest prison in the U.S. and is considered to be the most violent. Nicknamed "The Farm" because of its agriculture complex, it is the only maximum-security prison for men in Louisiana. Inmates earn between four cents and twenty cents an hour to do farm work and light industrial labor. The facility has been featured in movies such as *Dead Man Walking* and *Monster's Ball*.

Angola was once a plantation farmed by slaves. Its name derives from the designation for the west coast of Africa south of the Congo claimed by Portugal. The word itself is a Portuguese corruption of the Bantu word *Ngola*. Built on 18,000 acres of fertile farmland and manicured lawns, the façade of the institution belies what is inside. Elaine Cassel writes, "Angola used to be the bloodiest prison in America. Entering inmates had to learn how to protect themselves from other inmates. Deaths at the hands of guards, or literally from being worked to death in the fields, were not uncommon. For a time before [Warden] Cain arrived, Angola was under government supervision due to extreme violations of prisoners' civil rights by state guards and wardens" (Cassel 2000). The editors of Angola's award-winning, prisoner-produced magazine, *The Angolite*, give an even more poignant description of the environment there:

> The fabric of life in Angola was woven by the thread of violence. The only law was that of the knife, and the only protection available to you was what you could acquire through sheer force of character and the ability to impose your will upon others. Slavery was widespread and human life was the cheapest commodity on the market. (Griffin and White 2004)

There is no institution in the U.S. that embodies the hatred, callousness, and insensitivity of policymakers more than Angola. Some 85 percent of those sent there will die there. Louisiana has the harshest punishment laws in the U.S. While other states have a limit of 40 years for rape, for example, Louisiana has a limit of 75 years. Even Warden Burl Cain thinks the state's sentencing laws are outrageously harsh. Imagine doing 75 years of time in Louisiana for the same crime you would serve 5 years for in Idaho. Louisiana juries, made up mostly of whites, impose maximum sentences on convicted defendants, who are mostly black. There is no mercy in Louisiana when it comes to incarcerating and—in effect—ending the lives of black men. Angola is representative of America's deep-rooted disdain for young black rebels.

Although Angola has tried to rehabilitate its image in recent years, its legacy is one of brutality, injustice, and gross inhumanity. It too has embraced the same ugliness of the Stalinist gulags. With its vicious human rights abuses and history of corruption and violence, the Angola prison would fit very well in any country where human-rights violations are common—including Saddam Hussein's Iraq. The U.S. democracy cannot be a shining model for the world unless all its own institutions embrace justice and respect for human rights. The Angola prison has repeatedly violated the Eighth Amendment of the U.S. Constitution. It has engaged repeatedly in the exercise of meting out "cruel and unusual punishment" to its inmates, the majority of whom have been black.

The Walter Rideau story is a vivid example of the insensitivity of Louisiana's criminal justice system to black men. In 1961, Rideau—a 19-year-old high-school dropout—robbed a bank and kidnapped three employees. He shot two of his captives as they were running away; and in a state of panic, he stabbed and killed the third captive, a white woman. According to his testimony, he did not intend to murder the woman. Three all-white juries convicted Rideau of murder. The case polarized the town of Lake Charles along racial lines. Blacks put pressure on the local justice system to retry Rideau. The town complied. In 2000, a federal appeals court said Rideau's original 1961 indictment was flawed because blacks were excluded from the grand jury.

After serving 44 years, Rideau—who had become an award-winning journalist while in prison—was released from Angola in 2005. A jury of eight whites and four blacks re-heard his case. They found Rideau guilty of manslaughter rather than murder, because they concluded his killing of the woman was not premeditated. The maximum penalty for manslaughter in Louisiana is 21 years. Thus Rideau served more than twice the maximum time for the crime he committed (Associated Press 2005[a]).

I interviewed a very insightful inmate who served time in Angola during the 1990s. He was among the fortunate 15 percent who do not die there. He called Angola a "different world" and added, "The place brought out the worst in human nature." He said that as an inmate, he always had to be "strapped"—equipped—with a "shank"—a sharp weapon. "In Angola you have to let cats know that you are willing to die to protect yourself. If they don't see that 'I don't give a fuck' attitude you will be eaten alive in there" (Prison Inmate 2004). This former Angola inmate went on to tell me how the authorities do not view the inmates as human. He told me about the black men known as the Angola Three: Albert Woodfox, Robert King Wilkerson, and Herman Wallace.

Woodfox and Wallace, founders of the only officially recognized Black Panther group in a prison in the U.S., were said to be framed for the killing of a white prison guard in 1972. Since that time, they have had limited contact with visitors and limited access to medical care. They have consistently been denied due process and classification hearings. They have been kept in solitary confinement for more than thirty years, caged like animals in a 6-by-9-foot cell in the administration segregation unit of Angola that is known as the "hole." Wilkerson—like Woodfox, a former Black Panther—was released in 2001 after being confined in solitude under closed cell restriction for twenty-nine years. He proved before he left prison that he had been falsely accused (Griffin and White 2004).

Anita Roddick, the founder of The Body Shop who is also a writer and human-rights activist, traveled to Angola to interview Woodfox. She said that in the five hours they spent together Woodfox intrigued her with his comprehensive insights on issues ranging from corporate globalization to AIDS in Africa. Roddick writes:

> Albert described his cell for me: less than three metres square, it has a steel bed platform bolted to one wall with a thin mattress atop it. A small table is bolted to the opposite wall, and the third wall is occupied by a combination toilet and sink. He is not allowed to put anything on the walls, so he lines the perimeter of his wall with books along the floor. And he has two steel boxes under the bed in which he keeps all of his earthly belongings. He spends 23 hours a day there. Three days a week he is given an hour in the "yard," not much more than a small cage with a dirt floor, where he can exercise alone. The other four days a week, he can use his hour for a shower or to walk along the cramped cellblock. (Roddick 2002)

In the latter part of 2004, Herman Wallace was sentenced to Angola's Camp J, a unit known for its extreme conditions of isolation and deprivation. An inmate can be sent to Camp J for a number of arbitrary reasons. Wallace was thrown back into the dark dungeon only five months after his release from a two-year stint there. Angola is overcrowded and relies on keeping 400 inmates locked up in Camp J because there is not enough room to house the entire inmate population of 5,200 in the main facility. Imagine placing someone in an extreme punishment unit merely because there are no beds available elsewhere. Where is the justice in this exercise? The Angola 3 Support Committee asks the poignant question, "What is the difference between Abu Ghraib and Angola?" The Angola Three have filed a suit against the prison facility charging that Angola has violated the cruel and unusual punishment clause of the Eighth Amendment. In the summer of 2004 the U.S. Supreme Court agreed to hear this case (Angola 3 Support Committee 2004).

I interviewed Sergeant Michael Hughes, a correctional officer who worked in Angola State Prison in the 1990s before continuing his career in the California system. His job at Angola was his first experience as a correctional officer. After only one week on the job, he was called out to the farm because of an emergency. He will never forget what he saw when he arrived on the scene. An older inmate, who was working in the field cutting weeds with a swing blade, had made advances to a young, newly arrived inmate. When the young man fiercely resisted, the older inmate swung the blade at the young man's head. The blow decapitated him. When Hughes arrived on the scene, he saw a body and a head about six feet apart. Blood spewed from both parts, and the body of the young man jerked for minutes (Hughes 2004).

During another interview with Hughes, I asked what it was like, going to work every day at Angola. He said that you have to take a deep breath before you go in the gates. You have to prepare yourself mentally each day. Death permeated the air of the prison and made the entire environment toxic. "As soon as you walk in the gates," he said, "you smell death ... as you walk around you feel death all around you ... it's hard to describe that feeling to people" (Hughes 2005).

Prison Rape

U.S. Defense Secretary Donald Rumsfeld has called the abuse of Iraqi prisoners at the notorious Abu Ghraib prison "un-American." Surely this description resonates with people across the United States who are appalled by the pictures and reports of inhumane abuses, many of which are sexual in nature. But, as we puzzle over this as a nation, one phenomenon that must be examined is the rampant sexual abuse that has flourished in U.S. prisons for decades. When viewed through this lens, the abuse in Iraq—while still unconscionable—is much less surprising. (Stop Prison Rape Organization 2004)

Hughes recounted the first time he witnessed a rape at Angola. His responsibility at the time was to do an evening count in one of the dorm cells. As he approached the shower, an inmate stopped him to ask random questions. After five minutes of answering the inmate's questions, Hughes suspected something was not right, that the inmate was trying to block his way. In the shower area he saw two inmates engaged in sex. One had overpowered the other. It was an animalistic scene. Hughes added, "it made me sick to my stomach" (Hughes 2004).

I asked him about the prevalence of prison rape. He told me it depends on the facility. The California prisons, according to Hughes, are more civil than those in the South. Ironically, this civility and the lower incidence of prison rape in California are the results of existing gang infrastructure. The various gangs construct the informal rules and regulations of prison life. Some Mexican gangs have existed since the 1940s, and some black gangs are now in their third generation. If you are affiliated with a gang when you enter prison in California, you have some amount of protection from sexual predators (Hughes 2004).

Scant protection exists at Angola. Shana Griffin and Brice White describe life there:

> Rape and murder were ways of life. Sex slavery kept inmates under control with weak and young inmates being bought and sold by those older and stronger. Armed prisoner guards ran the facility as the budget did not allow for enough "free men" to control the thousands of men incarcerated at Angola. Disputes were settled by violence, often ending in death. Prison officials knew that keeping the men fighting between each other made their job of control possible. (Griffin and White 2004)

Sergeant Hughes observed that it was about "Charles Darwin in Angola ... straight survival of the fittest." In his estimation, at least 80 percent of the inmates who enter Angola "get turned out"—raped. "The way it works" says Hughes, "is that when guys come in there are a host of brothers who are picking and choosing as they enter the cellblocks." In order to get protection, the newly arrived inmate has to form an allegiance with someone. This person will act as his pimp. The "soft" approach of talking and getting to know the newcomer is used first. If this does not work, the predator resorts to the "hard" approach, involving intimidation, force, and violence. After the newcomer is "broken" he has to pay his pimp rent in the form of money, items from the canteen, or sex. According to Hughes—the former Angola guard—"There might be someone in another cellblock who wants sexual favors with your new team member. He might want to even buy him from his pimp. Everything is for sale. The new inmate can be sold to someone for three cartons of cigarettes." I asked if anyone could be turned out. Hughes looked me in the eyes and said, "Anyone. It doesn't matter about your size, muscles, education, or status on the outside. Anyone can be turned out. Basically what you have in facilities like Angola is a pimps and hoes subculture. You're either a pimp or you're someone's bitch" (Hughes 2005).

According to Hughes, in a cellblock you know who the prison pimps are because they usually have a lot of guys hanging around their bunks. A prison pimp has inmates on his team who will help break down other inmates. In a place such as Angola, there are dorm cells that house up to seventy inmates. The pimp might instruct one of his team members to take one of the newcomers into the shower and break him. Right after the new inmate breaks, the pimp enters the shower. There are guards on duty in the cell around the clock, so a "game" is run on the guard whose job it is to monitor the cell dorm. As the guard walks to the end of the cell dorm that is farthest from the shower, a "point man" moves toward the shower. When the guard approaches, the point man leaves, signaling to those inside that the guard is nearing the shower area. By the time the guard arrives at the shower, an inmate has been overpowered and raped. The point man is usually compensated with something like cigarettes for his trouble.

Hughes estimates that almost 100 percent of the inmates at Angola are involved in some form of sexual intercourse and attributes this to the culture of the place. In California, inmates use threats, intimidation, and violence to get money or material benefits. They are not preoccupied with sex. In Angola, sex is the predominant occupation of inmates. He says, "In Angola just because you fight a cat off of you one night doesn't mean you've won. It's a constant struggle, everyday. Every night you close your eyes you have to be on guard. If you're doing a lot of time it's a good chance that someone will eventually break you" (Hughes 2005).

In the California prison system, the primary victims of rape are inmates who arrive non-affiliated, meaning they have no ties to the prominent gangs. Without gang affiliation, there is little or no protection. A correctional officer told me the story of a young man who came to the Chino Institute for Men when he was 19 years old. He was non-affiliated but full of bravado. He began to act out towards the correctional officers to show the other inmates his toughness. He later claimed 5150, which is the California penal code for mental illness. The correctional officers put this inmate in the administration segregation unit for his unruly behavior. After a period of five months, one of the inmates tapped the young man on the shoulder and said, "Your act has played out." The non-affiliated 19-year-old was brutally raped by the other inmate. The officer I interviewed said he took the young man to the prison hospital and had never seen anyone torn up like that (CIM Correctional Officer 2004).

During my research I learned of another case of prison rape that took place in the Chino facility. The wife of a non-affiliated Mexican immigrant inmate came to see him every weekend. One weekend, however, he refused to come out of his cell. The correctional officers could not get him to budge so they brought in a counselor, who learned his cellmate had overpowered and raped him between his wife's visits. The inmate did not want to see his wife because he felt less than a man. Cellmate rape is the most common form of rape in the California system. As the CIM correctional officer said to me, "Who can they tell?" Indeed, a victim of cellmate rape is in a terrible position. If he tells other inmates he was raped, he is admitting he is weak and can be overpowered. This makes him susceptible to other attacks. If he tells a guard or someone else in authority, he is branded a snitch and opens himself up to other retaliation. So most inmates who are sexually assaulted in prison stay silent. But it's hard to disguise cellmate rape in the open-bar cells. As one correctional officer stated to me, "The rest of the inmates hear the groans in the middle of the night, then the word spreads" (CIM Correctional Officer 2004).

Inmates sometimes change cells covertly, giving predators free reign. As they come and go through the system and guards shift from one prison yard to another, some inmates slide into the cell of the person they want to assault. There is usually a payoff arranged for the victim's regular cellmate to switch to another cell for the night. When the correctional officers do their nightly counts, they are concentrating on the bodies in the cell rather than the identification of the inmates housed there.

In some cases, prison officials are blatantly responsible for inmate rape. The punishment for a belligerent inmate might be to put him in a cell with an inmate known to be a sexual predator. Employing this kind of punishment is a shameful human rights violation. The fact that rape is so prevalent in U.S. prisons is itself a major violation of human rights. There are serious consequences that result from this behavior, as one U.S. Supreme Court Justice has noted:

> The horrors experienced by many young inmates, particularly those who are convicted of nonviolent offenses, border on the unimaginable. Prison rape not only threatens the lives of those who fall prey to their aggressors, but it is potentially devastating to the human spirit. Shame, depression, and a shattering loss of self-esteem accompany the perpetual terror the victim thereafter must endure. (Blackmun 1994)

Angola's culture of sexual exploitation, however extreme, is a reflection of a serious issue that exists behind the "iron curtain." There has been no comprehensive research conducted about prison rape in the U.S. In the 1994 case, *Farmer v. Brennan*, the U.S. Supreme Court ruled that deliberate indifference to the issue of sexual assault behind prison walls violates rights established by the Eighth Amendment. Many rapes are never reported, but the conservative estimate is that during the past two decades, more than one million inmates have been raped in prison. Approximately 13 percent of those incarcerated have been victimized by prison rape. Many have been assaulted multiple times. Mentally ill inmates are at increased risk, as are young, first-time offenders. Young offenders are at least five times more likely to be raped in adult prisons than they are in juvenile facilities. Many juvenile offenders are raped within 48 hours of incarceration. Prison personnel are not adequately trained to deal with the physical and psychological consequences of prison rape (U.S. Congress 2003).

There is serious and justified concern about HIV/AIDS in prison facilities. In 2000, 25,088 inmates were reported to have HIV/AIDS. Some 6 percent of the deaths in federal and state prisons are due to this disease. The increased risk of tuberculosis and hepatitis B and C transmitted through prison rape also poses serious health risks. In 2003, Congress passed the Prison Rape Elimination Act, something that should have been done decades ago. This Act "provides for the analysis of the incidence and effects of prison rape in Federal, State, and local institutions and to provide information, resources, recommendations, and funding to protect individuals from prison rape" (U.S. Congress 2003, 1).

Among the consequences of prison rape is the spread of disease when infected inmates reenter society. Numbers of parolees and ex-offenders have brought diseases such as HIV/AIDS back into the black community. This has had a devastating effect. Black men going through the revolving door of prisons have contributed significantly to the spread of HIV/AIDS among African Americans. Overall, the statistics on the African American population infected with HIV/AIDS relative to the white population are startling. AIDS now kills more African Americans than any other disease. From 2000 to 2003, in thirty-two states, blacks made up more than half of new AIDS cases despite the fact that they represent less than 13 percent of the population. Black men have an HIV/AIDS rate nearly seven times that of white men. Black women are thirteen times more likely to be infected with HIV/AIDS than white women (Windsor 2005).

Prison Overcrowding

In 2005 I had the pleasure of speaking to a team of academics from Bulgaria and a group of utilities managers from China. Both the Bulgarians and the Chinese wanted to get a fundamental understanding of the dynamics of public policy in the U.S. I gave each group the same lecture and the same explanations. I told them that only two components of the public policy process are actually focused on public policy. These are implementation and evaluation. The other components—setting agendas, formulating policy, making decisions—are political in nature.

The two groups came to the U.S. expecting to study an exemplary model. I gave them a different perspective on how U.S. public policy is made. In many ways, I stated, this nation's public policy process is less than admirable. The power elite disproportionately influences a process that is woven tightly around initiatives that are politically expedient and profit-oriented. They are often not in the best interests of the public. I used examples from the criminal justice culture to make my points. How do corrections policies that focus solely on punishment instead of rehabilitation—and contribute to high recidivism rates—serve the public interest? How does building more prisons and fewer universities serve the public interest?

Overcrowded prisons in the U.S. are the consequence of terribly flawed public policy. They do nothing positive for our society. These facilities create dangerous environments for correctional officers as well as for inmates. Lawmakers have energetically moved to incarcerate thousands of individuals without a blueprint for how these individuals are to be housed. Is it in the best interest of U.S. society for lawmakers to punish nonviolent offenders harshly, with lengthy sentences? Is there logic in locking up a nonviolent offender for a very long time because of the possession of a small amount of an illegal drug? Is this a wise use of taxpayers' money? Prisons throughout the U.S. are overcrowded because of flawed logic and an absence of creativity, courage, and vision.

The California state assemblyperson from my district came to my university to speak to students about her roles and duties in the legislature. During the part of the roundtable discussion reserved for questions, I asked what she was doing about counterproductive corrections policies in the state. She looked at me and stated, with a set expression, "I cannot appear to be soft on crime. My constituents want me to be tough on offenders." I asked, "What about doing what's right?" She answered that she was chosen to carry out the will of the people. This assemblyperson's response oversimplifies the process of a representative democracy. In our system, we choose representatives to make wise and just decisions for the public good. It is my assemblyperson's job to educate her constituents about the negative impact on their shared community of hyper-punitive corrections policies. It is her responsibility to let her constituents know it is in their best interest to rehabilitate inmates rather than merely punish them. It is her responsibility to tell her constituents that public safety is threatened when recidivism rates are high. With her flawed logic, my state assemblyperson has contributed to overcrowded prisons.

From 1974 to 2001 there was a 574 percent increase in the U.S. prison population. Since 1980 alone it has quadrupled and now stands at two million. This population costs $60 billion to manage (Elsner 2004). The states with the most people incarcerated are Texas, Florida, California, New York, Michigan, Georgia, Illinois, Ohio, Colorado, and Missouri. Since 1979, these states have tripled the number of prisons they operate and now house 31 percent of the nation's correctional facilities (Kantor 2004).

All of the 32 correctional facilities in California are overcrowded. The least crowded facility is at 139 percent of intended capacity and the most overcrowded is at an appalling 249 percent of intended capacity. What are the consequences of such overcrowding? Dayrooms, which were meant to be used for leisure activities—watching television and playing games such as Ping-Pong or cards—are now used in California to house inmates. These rooms are being filled with double and triple bunk beds and lockers where inmates can store their belongings. The inmates put in these new spaces are usually the ones transferred from county jails. Anyone struggling to gain peace of mind and solitude would find these noisy and overcrowded arrangements extremely challenging. As Fred Steed states about the Georgia state prison where he was incarcerated, "The living conditions were tight and smoggy at all times. There were over 100 men in my dorm and 85 percent of them smoked. It was tough to inhale smoke almost 24 hours a day" (Steed 2004).

The dramatic increase in the prison population during the past two decades is largely due to the misdirected War on Drugs. During this period, both liberal and conservative politicians scrambled to show their constituents that they were tough on crime. One manifestation of this was the Prison Litigation Reform Act (PLRA) of 1996.

This "reform" act made it harder for inmates to charge officers with abuse and mistreatment. For example, a correctional officer might falsely accuse an inmate of possessing contraband, or drugs. If the charge is filed and validated, an inmate will likely receive more time added to their sentence. The PLRA made it more difficult for inmates to challenge false accusations; as a consequence, it made it more difficult for them to challenge extended sentences. This act was the result of the increasing number of lawsuits filed by inmates who alleged civil rights abuses and other violations. During the six years following the enactment of PLRA, inmate lawsuits decreased by 43 percent while the prison population increased by 23 percent (Vogel 2004).

Other variables also contribute to prison overcrowding, some of which are highlighted elsewhere in this book. Parolees and probationers are returned to prison for minor technical violations such as missing curfew or being late to a meeting. Mandatory minimums and three strikes laws keep inmates incarcerated for unduly long periods. There is also a flawed defense system for indigents. In Louisiana, public defenders have caseloads that are six times that recommended by the American Bar Association. Across the country, public defenders are overloaded, which clogs the jails with individuals waiting for trial.

In the 1990s many states passed laws requiring inmates to serve a specific and substantial portion of their sentences. Inmates in California, for example, were required to serve 85 percent of their time. Rules passed in Georgia in 1998 required inmates convicted of any one of twenty offenses to serve 90 percent of their time. When asked about reversing this policy to ease overcrowding in prisons, Georgia parole board member Eugene Walker stated, "It's so political.... We don't want to give nobody the impression that we're going soft on crime" (Campos 2004, A1).

Concerned with prison overcrowding and fairness, in late 2004 New York—the state that pioneered mandatory minimum sentencing—moved to revise tough drug policies, joining twenty-one other states working to make drug laws more reasonable (Marks 2004, 2). Why did it take New York thirty years to officially acknowledge the fundamental flaws in their harsh drug laws? During that time, these irrational laws caused irreparable damage to the lives of thousands of nonviolent criminals and their families.

From a policy perspective, prison overcrowding is just one consequence of unforgiving and shortsighted public policies.

Prison Corruption

Corruption is widespread throughout correctional facilities in the U.S. It permeates the upper levels of corrections administration and extends to the behavior of correctional officers. It is the prison guards who are ultimately responsible for the implementation of corrections policies. Because of the nature of their jobs, it is tremendously difficult to reduce their autonomy and discretion. The potential for corruption always exists when individuals in such positions possess high degrees of autonomy and discretion.

Corcoran State Prison in Corcoran, California, was designed to accommodate 2,916 prisoners. It now has an inmate population that exceeds 4,800. Its mission statement reflects a compassion that is unique in the field of corrections.

> The California State Prison-Corcoran is committed to ensuring and instilling the public and inmates' families with the confidence that CSP-C is committed to providing the best medical, mental health, education, vocational and self help programs for all inmates confined to Corcoran. CSP-Corcoran not only meets this commitment by providing its employees with the proper training, tools and safe working environment, but also by encouraging ideas and collaboration between all departments. (California Department of Corrections 2004)

At least on paper, this prison facility has espoused a humane corrections philosophy. Its mission statement certainly does not reflect the callous and insensitive rhetoric commonly found in the 1980s and 1990s. Perhaps years of blatant misconduct by Corcoran's prison guards forced the institution to embrace a more sensitive approach. Between 1989 and 1995, Corcoran guards shot fifty Security Housing Unit prisoners. Seven were killed. Guards participated in brutal and violent activities for entertainment. The fatal shooting of inmate Preston Tate in 1994 compelled federal authorities to investigate the facility. Guards arranged a fight for Tate so they would have a reason to shoot him. He was shot dead at close range by a guard because he was fighting (Wisely 2003, 245).

In May of 2005, African American Raymond Smoot, an inmate in an overcrowded jail at the state-run Baltimore Central Booking and Intake Center, was beaten to death by guards. Six guards were placed on leave after the incident. Smoot had been at the facility for about ten days after being charged with theft. When a guard had difficulties getting the 52-year-old Smoot back into his cell, a struggle broke out. Twenty-five to thirty guards were involved. Smoot was beaten and stomped to death by the guards, and his death was ruled a homicide by the state medical examiner's office. Since 2002, twenty-seven inmates have died at this Baltimore center. The facility was intended to process up to 45,000 people a year but now receives more than 100,000 people annually. Cells designed to hold five to eight people are occupied by as many as eighteen inmates. At the Baltimore center, "Some people nap under toilets. Sick people without medications get sicker, sometimes vomiting on others" (Associated Press 2005[b], 1).

As a rule, prison guards tend to have adversarial relationships with inmates. There are exceptions, as Quake Fisher points out in Chapter Three. But a substantial number of guards believe in a punishment-only philosophy. Those who embrace this mindset despise initiatives to rehabilitate inmates. As the staff director for the California State Senate Government Oversight Committee looking into prison abuse states, "Prison administrations are less in control of what is going on inside their prisons than are the guards who are not interested in promoting rehabilitation" (Wood 2004, 2). The California correctional officers union, one of the most powerful interest groups in the state, has a vested interest in opposing inmate rehabilitation. High recidivism rates translate into job security for prison guards. Nevertheless, after years of scandalous activities in the California prison system, authorities have begun to push for reforms. Indeed, the 2005 name change from the California Department of Corrections to the California Department of Corrections and Rehabilitation, signals reform.

Prison guards, like many police officers, share backgrounds and profiles similar to the individuals they manage and police. Some prison guards were gang-affiliated in their youth and were just one bad decision away from being behind bars themselves. For example, in the late 1990s some of the prison guards in the Pelican Bay facility in Crescent City, California, formed a gang known as "Green Wall"— "GW"—or "7/23." The warden was said to have known of the gang's existence. The mentality of GW members mirrored that of prison gang members. GW is said to use its influence to smuggle drugs into prisons. Its name has been found scratched into institutional property in various California facilities.

In January 2004, California correctional employees testified under oath about the systematic abuses in the California Department of Corrections (CDC). In two days of hearings held by the California State Senate Select Committees on Government Oversight and the California Correctional System, politicians became aware of California's version of Abu Ghraib. Co-convener State Senator Jackie Speier, Democrat from San Mateo, opened the hearings by stating, "Much of the testimony we will hear will be startling and even unbelievable. Many whistleblowers who will speak under oath today fear for their jobs and their lives." Co-convener Gloria Romero, D-Los Angeles, said in her opening remarks, "California's prison system teeters on the brink of being declared bankrupt, not only in its policy but in its morality, starting with top prison brass" (James 2004). Romero referred to the findings spelled out in the conclusion of the 85-page Hagar Report. John Hagar was the "special master" appointed by a federal court judge in San Francisco to investigate the CDC. His report began by identifying the problems at the Pelican Bay prison facility and proceeded to document a long list of problems in the CDC, many of which were attributed to the highest levels of administration (James, 2004).

Hagar also exposed the CDC code of silence. Under this unspoken but widely accepted code, CDC employees conspired to keep silent about the corrupt practices of co-workers. Playing by the rules of the code often meant making false statements to investigators in order to protect fellow employees. According to Hagar, "the most egregious form of the code is lying in federal court."

Employees who violate the code are isolated, ostracized and labeled "rats" or "snitches." But the ramifications go beyond name-calling; getting such a label can mean that in the case of a prison altercation or riot, backup assistance from co-workers might not be there. "A minority of rogue officers can establish a code of silence, threaten the majority, damage cars, isolate uncooperative co-workers, and create an overall atmosphere of deceit and corruption," Hagar wrote. "It cannot be emphasized too strongly that the code of silence is always accompanied by corruption." (James 2004)

The Mississippi State Prison known as Parchman sits on approximately 18,000 acres of land. It opened in 1901 and remains the state's oldest and biggest prison facility. Like Angola in Louisiana, Parchman is Mississippi's only maximum-security prison. Some 4,700 inmates are held in ten different housing units. The conditions at Parchman, like those at Angola, constitute a human rights violation. In 2003, U.S. Magistrate Jerry Davis ordered the state to improve conditions at Parchman. While his report focused only on physical conditions, the judge should have highlighted as well the rampant corruption at Parchman. Davis stated that conditions there "constitute cruel and unusual punishment in violation of the Eighth Amendment." The federal judge ordered the Mississippi Department of Corrections to take ten actions to remedy the problems, including annual mental health checkups, better lighting, improved toilets, insect control, and ways to keep inmates cool during the summer heat.

Mississippi State House Penitentiary Committee Chairman Bennett Malone (D-Carthage) disagreed with the federal judge's findings. He warned people not to jump to any conclusions. Malone, fearing the enormous costs required to implement Judge Davis's orders, stated, "I'm not sure it's as bad as it appears to be." He continued, "You hope that all the interested parties will sit down and use a lot of common sense to work this out." A 24-year legislative veteran, Malone is not enthusiastic about doing the right thing but chooses instead to do what is politically self-serving.

I became familiar with Parchman as a child. My father grew up in Jackson, Mississippi, and there are two institutions that are well known to everyone who lives in the state. One is Whitfield, the state mental institution; and the other is Parchman. When my heroin-addicted uncle-in-law killed my aunt in the 1970s, this is where he was incarcerated for murder. Another uncle, Bobby Earl, also served time at Parchman. Bobby walked in on his girlfriend and her new boyfriend while she was gathering her clothes from his house to leave him. Bobby shot her five times. She was hospitalized for nearly a year before she died from her wounds. My grandmother went to visit Bobby at Parchman every second Sunday for almost six years. For this book, I asked her about her impressions of the prison. She said she rarely saw any whites there. If she had to guess, she said she thought it was at least 90 percent black. Bobby, a Vietnam War veteran, had never held a steady job. He received a substantial monthly check from the Veterans Administration that continued to come to him even after he was incarcerated. Because of this check, Bobby had considerable leverage in prison. A closet homosexual, Bobby was able to pay his prison pimp for protection and pay off guards for various benefits. He would often ask my grandmother to purchase watches and other items. I was shocked when she told me that she mailed, on different occasions, money to the private residences of correctional officers. She once sent $1,000 in cash to one home address. As I began to research more, I realized that this type of corruption is not uncommon.

In 2002, two correctional officers at Parchman were arrested for bringing drugs into the prison. The two incidents were unrelated. Both officers were charged with conspiring with inmates to distribute marijuana. In many cases, drugs are as available in prison as they are on the outside. I asked one correctional officer how this could be. He said that visitors, girlfriends, and wives bring the drugs in during visitation. He also stated that there were shady correctional officers who were a part of the problem.

I interviewed a parolee and asked him the simple question, "How do so many drugs get into the prisons?" He was candid in his response. He said there are three primary ways drugs come in. (1) They arrive in packages sent to inmates, hidden in other objects. (2) Girlfriends or wives bring them in on visits and inmates take them back to the yard by hiding them in their anal cavities. (3) Correctional officers bring in the drugs. This parolee stated, "Many of the correctional officers have the same gangsta mentality as the inmates."

According to this parolee, correctional officers can make a lot of money peddling drugs in prison. "A person can make about $50 off a dot of heroin, and one needle-size joint of marijuana can fetch $15." A correctional officer can make $1,500 from the same quantity of marijuana worth a couple of hundred dollars on the street. With so much money to be made and with the code of silence firmly in place, it is difficult to root out corruption in prisons (Parolee 2005).

References

Angola 3 Support Committee. 2004. Abu Ghraib or Angola State Prison. Accessed 17 December 2005 at http://neworleans.indymedia.org/news/2004/12/2605.php.

Associated Press. 2005[a]. Louisiana man returns home after nearly 44 years in prison. 17 January.

Associated Press. 2005[b]. Inmate dies after fight with guards. 16 May.

Blackmun, Harry. 1994. Supreme Court Case of *Farmer v. Brennan*. Accessed 5 May 2005 at http://www.spr.org/main.html.

Bush, George W. 2005. Presidential inaugural address, 20 January. Accessed 1 May 2005 at http://www.whitehouse.gov/inaugural/.

California Department of Corrections. 2004. California State Prison, Corcoran. Accessed 28 December 2004 at http://www.corr.ca.gov/InstitutionsDiv/INSTDIV/facilities/fac_prison_CORCORAN.asp.

Campos, Carlos. 2004. Packed prisons lead to talk about parole. *Atlanta Journal-Constitution*, 13 September.

Cassel, Elaine. 2000.The Angola prison rodeo. Review of *God of the Rodeo: The Quest for Redemption in Louisiana's Angola Prison* by Daniel Bergner. Accessed 21 May 2005 at http://college.hmco.com/psychology/resources/students/shelves/shelves_20000503.html.

CIM Correctional Officer. 2004. In-person interview regarding experience as a correctional officer in the Angola prison. Conducted at Chino Institute for Men, 1 November.

Elsner, Alan. 2004. America's prison habit. *Washington Post*, 24 January.

Griffin, Shana, and Brice White. 2004. Thirty-one years of resistance. Free the Angola Three. Accessed 25 May 2005 at http://www. prisonactivist.org/angola/31years.html.

Hughes, Mike. 2004. In-person interview regarding prison conditions in Angola. Conducted at Chino Institute for Men, 7 June.

Hughes, Mike. 2005. In-person interview regarding prison rape. Conducted at Chino Institute for Men, 7 February.

James, Stephen. 2004. The code of silence. National Review, 13 May. Accessed 20 April 2005 at www.newsreview.com/issues/sacto/2004-05-13/coverasp.

Jones, Tim. 2005. Amnesty International: Nations conflicted on rights group. Chicago Tribune, 1 June.

Kantor, Stu. 2004. Prison construction boom reaches 3 in 10 counties in states with greatest prison growth. Ascribe Newswire, 29 April.

Knowlton, Brian. 2005. Bush says jail report is "absurd," president also assails Democrats on Bolton. International Herald Tribune, 11 June.

Marks, Alexandra. 2004. More states roll back mandatory drug sentences. Christian Science Monitor, 10 December.

Parolee. 2005. In-person interview regarding prison corruption. Conducted in Pomona, CA, 13 April.

Prison Inmate. 2004. In-person interview about conditions in Angola prison. Conducted at Centinela State Prison, 22 October.

Roddick, Anita. 2002. Free the Angola Three. 4 March. Accessed 22 May 2005 at http://www.anitaroddick.com/readmore.php?sid=36.

Scheer, Robert. 2005. Blaming the messenger fools no one. Los Angeles Times, 7 June.

Steed, Frederick. 2004. Telephone interview regarding incarceration in the Georgia State Prison system. 30 July.

Stop Prison Rape Organization. 2004. Is sexual abuse in Iraq surprising? Accessed at http://www.spr.org.

U.S. Congress. 2003. Prison Rape Elimination Act of 2003.108th Cong., Public Law 108-79.

Windsor, Doug. 2005. National Black AIDS Day shows growing skepticism by African Americans. New York Bureau, www .365gay.com, 7 February.

Wisely, Willie. 2003. Corcoran: Sex, lies, and videotapes. In *Prison Nation: The Warehousing of America's Poor*, edited by Tara Herivel and Paul Wright. New York: Routledge.

Wood, Daniel B. 2004. California tackles its prison problem. *Christian Science Monitor*, 20 July.

Vogel, Richard D. 2004. Silencing the cells: Mass incarceration and legal repression in U.S. prisons. *Monthly Review* 56, no.1 (May).

Chapter 7

Corporate Crime

While young black men continue to be characterized as volatile and dangerous menaces to society, there are some corporations that are invisible perpetrators of the most egregious and unconscionable crimes against humanity. These corporations serve the interests of the wealthy and powerful rather than those of the general public.

The Power Elite

Most people are not conscious of how their lives are affected by the wealthy class in this country. They are too immersed in their daily routines to contemplate how they are controlled by the privileged few. But it is impossible to understand the public policy process in the U.S. without understanding the dynamic influence of the elite class, whose primary objective is to support public policies that first protect and then expand their wealth.

While visiting the traumatized evacuees of Hurricane Katrina in the Houston Astrodome, Barbara Bush, captured what seems to many to be the sentiment of the elite: "Everyone is so overwhelmed by the hospitality. And so many of the people in the arena here, you know, were underprivileged anyway, so this is working very well for them." This "let them eat cake" statement exposed an elitist mindset that enraged many (Associated Press 2005, 3).

In his classic book, *The Power Elite*, C. Wright Mills writes, "The powers of ordinary men are circumscribed by the everyday worlds in which they live, yet even in these rounds of job, family and neighborhood they often seem driven by forces they can neither understand nor govern." Mills captures the powerlessness of the working class in America. "Great changes are beyond their control, but affect their conduct and outlook none the less. The very framework of modern society confines them to projects not their own" (1959, 3). A contemporary example that supports Mills's argument is the Iraq War. Although a majority of the American public was opposed to sending troops into Iraq to find weapons of mass destruction or effect regime change, we still went to war. The President and his cabinet—with the endorsement of Congress—went against public opinion. None of these decisionmakers was negatively affected by the war. Only one member of Congress had a child serving in the military at the time the war began. Hence, only one of the members of Congress who made the collective decision to endorse the war could suffer the despair and misery that comes from losing a son or a daughter in combat.

The top 0.5 percent of the U.S. population has consistently accounted for over 20 percent of the wealth in this country. This percentage has increased significantly in the past decade. Although corporations make billions of dollars, corporate taxes account for only 7 percent of the federal revenue stream (Kirst 2004). Elites are relatively invisible and their practices remain unexposed. According to G. William Domhoff, when the public thinks of the wealthy they tend to think of a few wealthy families—the Rockefellers, Mellons, and Du Ponts, for example—or celebrities such as entertainers and athletes. Rarely do they stop to think of the investment bankers, partners in large law firms, or directors of large foundations. These invisible people have an enormous impact on U.S. public policy. Domhoff characterizes this elite group:

> Members of this privileged class, according to sociological and journalistic studies, live in secluded neighborhoods and well-guarded apartment complexes, send their children to private boarding schools, announce their teen-age daughters to the world by means of debutante teas and gala ballroom dances, play backgammon and dominoes at their exclusive social clubs and travel all over the world on their numerous junkets and vacations…Some even involve themselves in the political fray, where they are referred to variously as "patricians," "Brahmins," "aristocrats" and "bourbons." (1978, 4)

Mills defines the concept of higher immorality as a **moral insensibility.** David Simon and D. Stanley Eitzen, authors of *Elite Deviance,* define higher immorality "as an aspect of the U.S. elite, a sort of systemic violation of the laws and ethics of business and politics" (1990, xiv). While street criminals are involved in murder, assault, theft, drug sales, drug possession, and check fraud, corporate criminals are immersed in bypassing tax laws, price fixing, price gouging, bribery, deceptive advertising, and fraud. Corporate criminals also produce hazardous products, pollution, dangerous working conditions, and resource waste, all of which could lead to health problems and early deaths for individuals. Fraud is at the core of corporate crime. "Fraud is committed when one is induced to part with money or valuables through deceit, lies, or misrepresentation. Although the law recognizes fraud as a crime, it has traditionally assumed that a fraud directed against a private individual is not a crime because of the principle of caveat emptor" (Simon and Eitzen 1990, 107). Ivan Preston characterizes **caveat emptor** in this way:

> The buyer must accept full responsibility for a sales transaction; the seller accepts none. He must rely upon and trust nothing but his own personal inspection of his purchase, ignoring any representations of the seller which he does not confirm for himself. Any buyer who does other than this must suffer all consequences of purchases which turn out badly. (Simon and Eitzen 1990, 107)

As stated in *Elite Deviance,* "in terms of economic costs, street crime is a minor problem when compared to illegal activities by corporations. To cite just one example, the $2 to $3 billion lost in Equity Funding fraud involved more money than the total losses of all street crimes in the United States for one year" (Simon and Eitzen 1990, 111).

Corporate Misconduct

Corporate deviants have taken an incalculable toll on our environment; indeed, corporate misconduct was the impetus for the environmental movement in the U.S. It was corporate insensitivity and carelessness toward the environment that prompted Rachel Carson to write her classic book *Silent Spring* in 1962.

The *New York Times* carried a front-page story about Love Canal on August 2, 1978. The Hooker Chemical Company had used the canal as an industrial-waste dump. The *Times* reported that after twenty-five years of dumping activity, "82 different compounds, 11 of them suspected carcinogens, have been percolating upward through the soil, their drum containers rotting and leaching their contents into the backyards and basements of 100 homes and a public school built on the banks of the canal." The Love Canal experience was the catalyst for the Comprehensive Environmental Response, Compensation, and Liability Act (CERCLA), more widely known as Superfund (Kraft and Furlong 2004, 33). No one from the Hooker Chemical Company was ever prosecuted for the destructive environmental practices that had such significant and negative long-term consequences for an entire community.

The film *Erin Brockovich* was based on a true story. As the film's promotional ad states, Brockovich, played by Julia Roberts, "brought a small town to its feet and a huge company to its knees." Brockovich, a poor single mother with three kids, helps win a monumental environmental law case against the giant corporation Pacific Gas and Electric (PG&E). This story is unique, because the Davids of the U.S. rarely beat the Goliaths. PG&E was found guilty of environmental misconduct after four decades of dumping 370 million gallons of cancer-causing chemicals into unlined ponds in Hinkley, California. Hexavalent chromium was the primary chemical found in the groundwater. This "chrome-6" has been known to be a cancer-causing chemical since the 1920s. It is especially dangerous to the lungs.

Corporate misconduct has permeated every aspect of American society. Eric Schlosser highlights the culpability of the fast food industry in his book, *Fast Food Nation*. With their enormous purchasing power, fast food chains have fundamentally changed how cattle are raised, slaughtered, and processed into ground beef. According to Schlosser, "These changes have made meatpacking—once a highly skilled, highly paid occupation—into the most dangerous job in the United States, performed by armies of poor, transient immigrants whose injuries often go unrecorded and uncompensated" (Schlosser

2002, 9). He highlights how the fast food industry has carelessly and insensitively embraced the spirit of caveat emptor:

> And the same meat industry practices that endanger these workers have facilitated the introduction of deadly pathogens, such as E. coli 0157:H7, into America's hamburger meat, a food aggressively marketed to children. Again and again, efforts to prevent the sale of tainted ground beef have been thwarted by meat industry lobbyists and their allies in Congress. (Schlosser 2002, 9)

How can the gross manipulation and exploitation of the American public not be seen as a crime against society? Corporate misconduct is significantly more detrimental to society than street crime. While carjackers, muggers, and gang members are featured almost every night on the news, corporate thugs are hiding behind the shield of invisibility. I asked students in my course on diversity and the criminal justice system why there was such disparity between the punishment of street thugs and that of corporate thugs. One student answered, "Because street thugs are seen as more of a menace to society. They are the ones that we see on the news every night so they are the ones that we are programmed to fear." This student's candid analysis was accurate. No one in America has been conditioned to fear the corporate chief executive officer who wears expensive suits. However, the universally benign image of the CEO belies the malignant nature of some of his (or her) actions. Corporate thugs negatively affect society's well-being in ways that defy understanding or excuse. In many cases, corporate crime actually causes street crime. As George Winslow states, "While some types of corporate crime directly encourage street crime, many have an indirect but equally devastating impact by creating social problems—such as poverty, unemployment, bad housing, and poor educational systems—that cause high rates of street crime" (2003, 52).

The overwhelming majority of the tough-on-crime laws enacted during the past two decades have been focused on street crime and minor drug offenses. Relatively few laws have been put in place to curb corporate crime. Why? This is the great charade of American society. Corporate crime has taken a far greater toll on our society than street crime, even gang warfare. For example, during the height of the

Crips and Bloods disputes in South Central Los Angeles during the early 1990s, news media and movie producers were intrigued with the violence. 'Hood films were produced showcasing violent themes. Broadcast and print media covered gang violence daily. At the same time, author Ralph Estes was conducting a powerful study on corporate crime. Estes estimated that in 1991, corporate crime cost the U.S. economy $2.4 trillion. He breaks this total down as follows: the cost of racial and gender discrimination, $165 billion; workplace injuries and accidents, $141.6 billion; deaths from workplace cancer, $274.7 billion; price-fixing, monopolies, and deceptive advertising, $1.1 trillion; cost of unsafe vehicles, $135.8 billion; cigarettes, $53.9 billion; injuries from other products, $18.4 billion; environmental costs, $307.8 billion; defense contract overcharges, $25.8 billion; income tax fraud, $2.9 billion; violations of federal regulations, $39.1 billion; bribery, extortion, and kickbacks, $14.6 billion; plus a variety of other costs (Winslow 2003, 44). Although Estes conducted his analysis more than a decade ago, his results are still riveting. Imagine the damage that corporate corruption does to our society today.

Jeffrey Reinman also identified a disturbing trend in American society in his insightful 1995 book, *The Rich Get Richer and the Poor Get Prison*. John Edwards spoke during the 2004 Presidential campaign about the existence of two Americas, one for the wealthy and one for the poor, one for the haves and one for the have-nots. Edwards exposed the myth of America's claim of equal opportunity for all. Indeed, Americans live by a double standard.

Classism

American democracy and capitalism revolve around classism, which is inextricably linked to elitism. When I discuss the subject of elitism in my classes, I ask my political science students how many of them would spend $30,000 a year on country club fees if they could afford to. The majority of students always see these fees as an exorbitant waste of money. Invariably a handful of students will say they do not think of it as a waste. I let the students who would not pay the

$30,000 speak first. They energetically discuss how the money could be better spent doing other things, such as helping the poor. I then ask my students who think the fees are not a waste of money to speak. Typically, some of these students come from wealthy backgrounds. They see the fees as an investment, as the cost of access to privilege. They comment that $30,000 can be made in one day with one tip on a hot stock; that job opportunities are discovered in such settings; that haves must connect with other haves to protect and expand their wealth. This exposes those who would not pay the fees to another perspective entirely. They glimpse another America, another world. Many who were initially opposed to paying large amounts for country club fees have a change of heart. They begin to see the benefits of this "investment."

I once attended a book signing at the home of a popular Los Angeles socialite. As I stood in the living room of the multimillion-dollar estate, eating expensive hors d'oeuvres and mingling with the Hollywood and political elite, I realized this was where deals were made. The ambitious district attorney and the popular defense attorney could reach casual consensus on criminal cases. These are the settings in which charges are dropped against, for example, a privileged college student caught by the authorities with a supply of crystal meth.

I routinely ask my students whether they think America is an open or closed society, whether a person can become anything they will themselves to be. Their knee-jerk response to my question is always something like, "Sure. You can be whatever you want to be in America. This is the land of opportunity. Anyone who is willing to work hard can achieve the American dream." This type of response reflects years of socialization, propaganda, and relative truth. I ask the question, "Can anyone in this room become President?" In a classroom filled with minorities, working-class students, and women, the consensus is that the answer is "No." The students realize that none of them could actually become President of the United States. Although we all might believe that America, relative to other nations, is an open society, this exercise drives home a poignant point. America is in fact elitist. As Domhoff states, "In a nation that always has denied the existence of social classes and class conflict, and overestimated the degree of social mobility, systematic information on the persistent inequality of wealth and income tends to get lost from public and academic debate" (1978, 7).

John Locke outlined in *Two Treatises on Government* that a social contract exists between the people and the government. The people agree to follow the government's rules and regulations in exchange for the government's protection. In this contractual relationship, citizens of the state are to be obedient and the government is to safeguard the natural and unalienable rights of life, liberty, and property. According to Locke, if the government fails to uphold its end of the contract the people have a right to replace it. The U.S. government is uniquely deceptive. Instead of protecting the rights of the people, it has opted to protect the rights of an elite few. Institutional structures have been put in place to benefit the elite class at the expense of the masses.

A commentary in *The Economist* characterizes how some in the U.S. view corporate crime:

> Thanks to a review of sentencing guidelines in 2001, further beefed up following directives in the Sarbanes-Oxley legislation adopted after the scandalous collapses of Enron and WorldCom, even junior executives found guilty of perpetrating corporate frauds are receiving lengthy prison sentences. Just punishment should strive to say that American justice is blind to color and wealth. Yet the current sentencing regime for company executives is troubling. The typical corporate crook has no prior convictions, will never again be put in a job where he can repeat the crime, and is usually a promising candidate for rehabilitation. A more specific worry is that the recommended sentences are too strictly defined and are too closely tied to the notion of the loss caused by a fraud. (2004, 17)

This commentary reflects a troubling mindset. It is ironic that the author would make a reference to justice being "blind to color and wealth," and then proceed to make the point that corporate crime is somehow innocent in nature. This author should visit the thousands of families who have lost their life savings because of corporate deviance. They have something to say about the current tough sentencing of corporate criminals. The writer of this commentary in *The*

Economist is clearly advocating lighter sentences with the words, "The typical corporate crook has no prior convictions...and is usually a promising candidate for rehabilitation." What makes a particular offender a "promising candidate for rehabilitation"? Perhaps first-time offender status. If this is the case, why are first-time offenders who are caught with five grams of crack sentenced to five years in prison? Why, under the tough War on Drug laws, do first-time offenders get sentenced to 15 years to life? If first-time corporate offenders are promising candidates for rehabilitation, then perhaps other first-time offenders are also.

Writer Herbert Hoelter echoes the sentiments of the commentary in *The Economist*. These likeminded sympathizers of corporate criminals have gone to great lengths to justify lenient sentences.

> Unpopular as it may sound, the most frustrating part of white-collar imprisonment is the incredible waste of resources. White-collar defendants, who pose virtually no risk of recidivism, are an incredible pool of talent...Given the tremendous needs of our society, spending $22,000 per year—the average cost of imprisonment—to have a white-collar defendant mow lawns or landscape the warden's house is ridiculous. (Hoelter 2002, 21A)

In Simon and Eitzen, however, sociologist Edwin Sutherland makes a counterpoint (1990, 111):

- The criminality of corporations tends to be persistent. Recidivism (repeat offenses) is the norm.

- The level of illegal behavior is much more extensive than the prosecutions and complaints indicate.

- Businesspeople who violate the laws designed to regulate business do not typically lose status among their associates. In other words, the business code does not coincide with the legal code. Thus, even when they violate the law, they do not perceive of themselves as criminals.

What industry has been more detrimental to our population than cigarette manufacturers? Tobacco company executives are among the most devious corporate criminals in our society. Yet until recently they received favorable treatment from lawmakers. Cigarette smoking has resulted in hundreds of thousands of deaths through the years. Cigarette makers entangled themselves in the political process by contributing large sums to the campaigns of many local, state, and national politicians. Generous campaign contributions effectively silenced any criticism. In 1999, under President Bill Clinton, a $280 billion lawsuit was filed by the government against all the major tobacco companies. In 2004 the case came to trial. Cigarette makers were accused of lying and confusing the public for five decades about the dangers of smoking. The government charged that cigarette companies participated in a conspiracy as far back as 1953, when a number of tobacco industry executives met at New York's Plaza Hotel to devise a strategy to obfuscate the link between smoking and cancer. Cigarette companies also refuted and worked actively to discredit the claim that smoking was addictive. Frank Marine, an attorney for the U.S. Justice Department, told a federal court, "This case is about a 50-year pattern of misrepresentation, half-truths, and lies by the defendants that continues to this day" (Kaplan 2004, 1).

Corporate Scandals

Ask the employee at Enron who has done more damage to his or her life, the crack fiend downtown or the corporate executive upstairs. While politicians were locking up crack users for five years for a first-time offense, they were allowing corporate criminals such as Charles Keating Jr. to cheat Americans out of hundreds of millions of dollars. Many politicians were on the same team as the corporate predators. Keating was an Arizona developer and owner of Lincoln Savings and Loan and its parent corporation, American Continental. He and his family and associates gave large sums in political donations. California's Governor Deukmejian received $188,464; the Republican Party, $100,000; and U.S. Senator Alan Cranston of California, $900,000. In exchange, Keating's companies received preferential treatment from state and federal regulatory agencies, which allowed them to sell $250 million in uninsured junk bonds that turned out to be worthless. Lincoln tellers were given bonuses to convince customers to move their savings from federally insured accounts to the worthless bonds (*San Francisco Chronicle* 1997).

After its investment scheme failed, American Continental filed for bankruptcy on April 13, 1989. Charles Keating was convicted on 73 federal counts of fraud, conspiracy, and racketeering, including swindling investors to invest in worthless junk bonds. He was sent to state prison in 1991, where he served four years and eight months. He spent ten years battling federal authorities about the validity of the charges brought against him before a plea bargain allowed a federal appeals court to overturn his convictions. The 75-year-old Keating was spared more jail time by pleading guilty to four counts of bankruptcy and wire fraud. He has been free since 1996. Prosecutors dropped charges that he had bilked thousands of elderly investors out of their life savings. The judge imposed no fines. There was no mandated restitution to the investors who lost $285 million, although they eventually won a $1 billion civil suit against Keating. It remains uncollected. The federal government won a judgment for $3 billion, the cost of bailing out Lincoln Savings and Loan (Reckard and Rosenzweig 1999).

Compare Keating's case to that of Gary Ewing. Keating was charged with 73 counts of criminal activity. He swindled millions of dollars from elderly and naive investors. After he admitted partial guilt, he was exonerated and his convictions were overturned. Ewing, not a choirboy, had a lengthy rap sheet of non-injurious felonies. These accounted for two strikes against him. Stealing three golf clubs worth a total of $399 was his third strike, and he was sentenced to 25 years to life in prison. The U.S. Supreme Court upheld this sentence, ruling it did not violate the cruel and unusual punishment doctrine of the Eighth Amendment. With its 5-4 decision, the Court said that Ewing's punishment was not disproportionate.

Those who maintain that the courts went easy on Keating because he was a septuagenarian must remember Martha Weatherspoon. At the age of 60, she was sentenced to 15 years to life for selling eight ounces of cocaine. She was in prison until she was 75 years old. What would social philosophers Rawls, Zinn, Kant, Mill, Hobbes, Locke, and Beccaria have to say about the justice Keating received compared with that meted out to Ewing and Weatherspoon? How were these crimes and punishment proportional?

Enron became the symbol of corporate crime in 2000. A Citibank loan for $8.5 million, disguised as commodity trades, allowed Enron to hide its losses and inflate the price of its stock. This ultimately led to the company's demise. Kenneth Lay, Jeffrey Skilling, Richard Causey, and Andrew Fastow were the key players in the Enron saga. Former CEO Lay faces eleven counts of fraud. Over a five-year period, he made $325 million in salary, stock options, and bonuses. Enron's manipulation of the energy market in 2001 paralyzed the entire state of California. Lay was charged with falsely representing the fiscal status of the company. Whistleblower Sherron Watkins was the Enron vice president who spoke up about massive accounting fraud. After this revelation the company's stock plummeted from $90 to $1 per share, causing 4,200 families to lose their retirement savings and pensions. Several years after he was indicted, Lay's trial is still pending as this book goes to press. Skilling, Enron's chief executive, was charged with nearly 35 counts of fraud, conspiracy, and insider trading. Taken together, these crimes added up to 325 years of prison time. Former chief accountant Richard Causey was charged with a number of criminal offenses, including fraud. Skilling and Causey's trials were still pending at the time of this book's publication. Fastow, formerly Enron's finance chief, was charged in 2002 with 78 counts of fraud, money laundering, and conspiracy. The U.S. Justice Department accused him of manipulating company financial results and hiding losses in secret partnerships. In a 2004 plea bargain, Fastow agreed to cooperate with prosecutors in exchange for a maximum sentence of 10 years (Sloan 2004; Huffington 2003). Employees of Enron who were not executives lost their life savings in this scandal. One long-time employee lost $700,000 in retirement funds (Romero and Desai 2004).

It was interesting to see Kenneth Lay being arrested and taken away in handcuffs. Corporate criminals are not usually pictured this way in the media. Imagine if all the corporate deviants who have swindled millions of dollars from investors were perpetually exposed by the media for their crimes and consistently shown being carted away in handcuffs. American media have bombarded our society with images of the black male deviant. Indeed, he has become the very symbol of crime—stealing, killing, pimping, drug using. While the Kenneth Lays of the country have been silently pillaging people's retirement accounts and ruining lives, the black man has been unremittingly demonized.

According to Michael Moore, every person who ever harmed him was white. He states that he has never been attacked by a black person, never had his security deposit ripped off by a black landlord, and never had a black person say, "We're going to eliminate ten thousand jobs here. Have a nice day" (Moore 2002, 57). Moore's analysis of white privilege is piercing.

> You name the problem, the disease, the human suffering, or the abject misery visited upon millions, and I'll bet you ten bucks I can put a white face to it...And yet when I turn on the news each night, what do I see again and again? Black men alleged to be killing, raping, mugging, stabbing, gang-banging, looting, rioting, selling drugs, pimping, ho-ing, having too many babies, dropping babies from tenement windows, fatherless, motherless, Godless, penniless... (Moore 2002, 59)

The corporate scandal at Adelphia, at one time the fifth-largest cable company in the nation, received less publicity than the scandal at Enron. This is because the crimes at Adelphia were revealed after Enron, and the company was smaller. Nevertheless, the arrogance, greed, and shiftiness displayed by the company owners parallel, if not exceed, the corporate games played at Enron. The trouble at Adelphia began in 2002 when a quarterly report revealed the company had borrowed more than $2 billion. The loan documents made the company and the family responsible for each other's debts. Founder and Adelphia CEO John Rigas and his son Timothy—Adelphia's chief financial officer—were the primary culprits. Adelphia executives testified that they routinely created numbers to give to investors and lenders. In 2004, a jury in federal court found 79-year-old John Rigas and his 48-year-old son guilty of cheating the company and its investors out of more than $100 million; hiding $2 billion in debt; and lying to the public about the company's operations and financial status. More specifically, the father and son were convicted of one count of conspiracy, fifteen counts of securities fraud, and two counts of bank fraud. Prosecutors in the case stated that they treated the company's money like "their own ATM machine." The company's excesses included paying for a collection of twenty-two cars for Timothy and his older brother Michael, and spending $6,000 to fly a Christmas tree to a family member. John and Timothy face up to 30 years in prison. Experts, however, say their sentences are likely to be reduced significantly (Grant and Nuzum 2004, A1).

Global Crossing, an international telecom carrier, came under scrutiny when it fixed its books and distorted revenue. CEO Gary Winnick offered to give $25 million of his own money to the employees who lost everything in the company's downfall. Those who knew that Winnick personally acquired $734 million before the company folded saw his gesture as a half-hearted public-relations ploy. Although federal investigators could not find sufficient grounds to file charges, there was clearly corporate deviance taking place (PR News 2004).

WorldCom CEO Bernard Ebbers was indicted on fraud charges similar to those filed against the executives at Enron and Adelphia. In 2002, in the wake of the Enron scandal, WorldCom, the nation's second-largest long distance carrier, revealed—under pressure from a federal investigation—that the company had distorted its financial status. WorldCom overstated its cash flow by more than $3.8 billion during a five-quarter period. This revelation forced the company to lay off 17,000 employees immediately in order to avoid bankruptcy. This had a devastating impact on the lives of 17,000 families (*New York Times Magazine* 2004). In 2005, Ebbers was convicted of conspiracy, securities fraud, and seven counts of filing false claims with securities regulators. Employees testified on behalf of thousands of their co-workers that they had lost their life savings because of Ebbers. He was sentenced to 25 years in prison for his fraudulent activities.

Tyco International, a company that makes a variety of products from health-care supplies to alarm systems, came under fire in 2002. CEO Dennis Kozlowski and chief financial officer Mark Schwartz were indicted by the Securities and Exchange Commission (SEC) for fraud and civil theft. These men were accused of giving themselves interest-free or low-interest loans for the purchase of personal property. These loans, according to the SEC, were never repaid. Under SEC rules, executives must alert investors when they sell shares of company stock. These two men failed to do so. Kozlowski and Schwartz were also accused of giving themselves bonuses without the approval of Tyco's board of directors. According to the Tyco Fraud Information Center, they were responsible for bilking Tyco out of millions of dollars. The first trial of Kozlowski and Swartz in 2004 ended in a mistrial. In a second trial in 2005, Kozlowski and Swartz were convicted of looting the company of more than $150 million. They face up to 30 years of prison time.

The credibility of once-reputable firms such as Merrill Lynch and Arthur Andersen has also been undermined by corporate crime. Merrill Lynch acknowledged betraying customer trust by skewing analyst reports to make some companies look healthy when they were not. Company executives were convicted in 2004 for helping Enron engage in fraudulent deals (Johnson 2005).

Chicago-based firm Arthur Andersen, once a pillar of the accounting industry, fell from grace in 2002. Some 28,000 employees lost their jobs when Andersen was found guilty of obstructing justice by destroying two tons of documents about Enron. Andersen's defense was that it was following standard company procedure by getting rid of all nonessential paperwork. This company procedure was implemented only six weeks after the SEC began investigating Enron's tangled finances. With a single ruling in 2005 relating to the Andersen case, the U.S. Supreme Court rescinded one of the biggest victories against corporate crime in the past decade. The Court ruled that Arthur Andersen was found guilty without proof that its shredding of documents was deliberately intended to undermine a looming SEC inquiry (Lane 2005).

Although there have been a few recent convictions for corporate malpractice, the process of prosecuting corporate crime has been entangled in mistrials, delays, postponements, deals, and settlements. Street criminals get prosecuted and sent to prison. They do not have the means to file for extensions and drag out their judgments. They do not have the luxury of coming up with sophisticated defenses or blaming their criminal behavior on their subordinates—as Richard Scrushy of HealthSouth did successfully.

Scrushy was the first chief executive charged with knowingly filing false financial statements under the Sarbanes-Oxley corporate governance law. Congress passed this comprehensive law to promote more honest and transparent accounting practices in the aftermath of the accounting frauds at Enron and WorldCom. It seemed, on paper, that the government had a strong case against Scrushy. Five former financial chiefs and fifteen other employees testified against him for carrying out a seven-year conspiracy that involved overstating earnings by $2.7 billion to boost shares and to enrich himself (Sachdev 2005). During the pre-trial phase of the proceedings, Scrushy and his wife launched an intensive public-relations campaign in Birmingham, Alabama, where they lived and where the trial would take place. Among other things, they held prayer vigils and worship sessions on one local television show. In the end, Scrushy's strategy paid off. After twenty-one days of deliberations, a Birmingham jury found Scrushy not guilty on 36 counts of fraud, conspiracy, money laundering, and other criminal activities.

Ivan Boesky, Michael Milken, and Leona Helmsley were the archetypical corporate criminals of the1980s. Their sentences reflected society's attitudes about their crimes. Boesky was convicted of insider trading in 1987. A federal judge approved a $68.9 million settlement requiring Boesky to repay investors who had been cheated by his securities fraud. He also served three years in prison (*New York Times* 1997). In 1988, the Securities and Exchange Commission charged Milken, the former junk-bond king, with multiple counts of securities fraud. He was sentenced to ten years in prison and served twenty-two months of his sentence. After his release, Milken faced three years of restrictions and 1,800 hours of community service (Norris 1998). Helmsley, a hotel magnate, was convicted of tax evasion in 1989 and sent to a federal prison in Danbury, Connecticut, on April 15, 1992. Her original sentence was a $7.1 million fine, thirty months in jail, three years on probation, and 750 hours of community service. After serving eighteen months in prison, she spent a month in a halfway house and two months under house arrest. Her probation was cut by nine months. She was still required to perform 750 hours of community service and pay millions of dollars for restitution, fines, back taxes, and penalties (James 1995).

In 2001, the U.S. Sentencing Commission revised its guidelines for white-collar crimes to stiffen, significantly, the penalties for fraud involving millions of dollars. Under the old guidelines, a person convicted of defrauding fifty or more people out of $100 million or more faced a prison sentence of only 5 to 6.5 years in a federal facility. Using the formula of the new guidelines, an individual convicted of the same offense will receive no less than 19.5 and no more than 24.5 years of prison time. According to the new guidelines, Michael Milken's sentence, for instance, would be double the one he received in 1990. Also, Milken's 10-year sentence was reduced to 22 months. The new guidelines prohibit federal parole and make it mandatory that an offender serve at least 85 percent of the sentence (Mitchell 2002). Perhaps some corporate criminals fear that the days of easy time, dramatically reduced sentences, and not-guilty verdicts for white-collar crime are gone. But lenient sentences and verdicts like Scrushy's prove that at least in some cases, corporate crime still pays.

Ten years is the benchmark for corporate crimes. If a person receives a sentence of more than 10 years, they will land behind razor wire. If the sentence is less than 10 years, they may land instead at a "Club Fed" facility (Mitchell 2002).

Club Feds

Can the penalties meted out to corporate criminals even be considered "punishment"? While street criminals suffer in overcrowded, triple-bunked, outdated facilities, white-collar criminals do their time in resort-like complexes pejoratively called Club Feds. Sam Waksal, the disgraced CEO of ImClone Systems, was convicted of securities fraud and cover-up in 2003 and sentenced to seven years in federal prison. Waksal's attorney boasted that he got the judge to grant his request for his client to serve his sentence at the Eglin Prison Camp in Florida. Eglin was rated by *Forbes* magazine as the best prison facility for white-collar criminals. Waksal's attorney announced that his client was hoping to bunk with fellow corporate crook Steve Madden. In 2001, shoe designer Madden pleaded guilty to conspiracy to commit money laundering and securities fraud. He was sentenced to 41 months at Eglin (*New York Times* 2002).

The Eglin Prison Camp is a minimum-security federal facility at Eglin Air Force Base, which is fifty miles east of Pensacola in Florida's Panhandle region. Eglin has been a federal institution since 1962 and is considered to be the model Club Fed prison. The pastoral campus, which sits on 28 acres, has four tennis courts, airy dormitories, and well-manicured lawns. A small number of guards oversee hundreds of low-risk prisoners.

There is no better place in the nation for an inmate to serve his time than at Eglin. Along with working on their tennis games, inmates can do yoga or make use of the private sunbathing beaches. As writer Dominic Rushe states, "The big difference between Eglin and Club Med seems to be that Eglin has no fences" (2003, 14). There are about 840 inmates living in a five-story dormitory-style facility. The median sentence is 94 months and the average age of inmates is 40. About 78 percent of those incarcerated at Eglin have been convicted of drug-related crimes. One of the requirements is working seven and a half hours a day for pay that ranges between 12 and 40 cents an hour. The prison has been the temporary home of Watergate figures E. Howard Hunt and H.R. Haldeman as well as former Maryland Governor Marvin Mandel (Dochat 2004).

Journalist Russ Mitchell argues that white-collar prison camp is still hard time and the myth about Club Fed is dashed when the inmates arrive. Since only 1,000 of the 160,000 federal inmates are corporate criminals—fewer than 1 percent—even Club Feds are populated by drug dealers, robbers, and check bouncers. David Novak, who spent nearly a year at Eglin as an inmate, said that his two-man room was the size of an office cubicle (Mitchell 2002). He recalls a Florida dentist arriving in his limousine. "His chauffeur removed golf clubs and a Louis Vuitton bag and walked in with him. The guard said, 'You can come inside, but tell your caddy he has to go home'" (McGhee 2003, K01).

There is a substantial difference between serving time in a federal prison facility and a state facility. In a federal prison there is no razor wire. No armed guards stare down from turrets at camps like Eglin. In most cases, there are no fenced boundaries. The landscape at Eglin resembles that at a college campus (McGhee 2003). State prisons are not so bucolic. There are also major differences inside the walls. Besides giving up one's freedom, sexual assault is the most intimidating aspect of going to prison. Prison rape is a part of the culture in many state institutions. However, this is not the case in federal facilities. "Newcomers often are terrified by the possibility of forced sex, but former inmates and prison officials agree that sexual assault in federal prisons is rare, even at the highest security levels, and practically unheard of in prison camps. Former inmates say that while officially forbidden, consensual sex is common and available," writes Mitchell (2002, 6).

The comparison of all federal prisons to resorts is an exaggeration. As Mitchell points out, "Almost no personal property is allowed, not even contact lenses. Inmates are allowed only one religious text, one pair of eyeglasses, dentures and dental bridge, one solid wedding ring with no stones, $20 in change for vending machines and cash or money orders for an inmate account" (2002, 6) Inmates can have as much money as they choose in their accounts, but they can only spend $175 per month. They can buy a small selection of goods such as tennis shoes, toiletries, and snacks in the commissary. This does not seem like the resort environment that some on the outside have described. Nevertheless, the environment at prisons like Eglin differs dramatically from the overcrowded, barbaric, and violent environment at many state prisons. Every human experience is relative to someone else's experience. The inmate in Angola living in a cell with three people but designed for one, who is continually assaulted and harassed, might consider a prison like Eglin to be resort-like, indeed.

There are few things in American life more emblematic of elitism than the policies and practices of the criminal justice system. If our liberal democracy truly lived up to the egalitarian spirit of the Constitution, there would be no racial or class disparities. In an ideal democracy, the arrest, conviction, and sentencing of an individual would not depend on their race, social network, political ties, or the amount of money they have in the bank. In the U.S., however, these factors determine an offender's fate. The 47 million Americans with federal or state criminal records constitute almost one-fourth of the adult population. However, those who are incarcerated are disproportionately poor and minority. The theft of a $300 bicycle is a crime against the state and society. The theft of $3 million is also a crime against the state and society. The punishment for each of these crimes should be proportional to the damage they cause. If the primary purpose of crime control is utilitarian, then corporate crime has taken a greater toll on society than street crime. If the primary purpose of crime control is retribution, then the corporate thief who steals $3 million should be required to pay back more than the street thief who steals $300. There is no justification or rationale for bias in an ideal democracy. Social philosopher John Rawls makes the argument that we should mete out justice by making decisions behind a veil of ignorance. This scenario is likely to remove bias from criminal justice policies and practices.

In the 1980s and 1990s street crime was fought fiercely and aggressively. The three strikes laws and the War on Drugs sent ordinary street criminals to prison for decades. A third strike, whether it was stealing an item of small worth, possessing marijuana, or committing check fraud, sent individuals to prison for 25 years to life. Tough drug laws sent small-time dealers and drug users to prison for 15 years to life. While the criminal justice system was overcrowding its prison facilities with young men from the inner cities, who was monitoring the corporate criminals?

Two films from the 1980s are reflective of the two Americas that John Edwards referred to in his campaign speeches. The 1987 film *Wall Street* starred Michael Douglas as Gordon Gekko, the greedy, power-hungry financial broker. His character is an example of the money-obsessed mindset of corporate executives in the1980s. The most memorable line of this Oliver Stone film—"Greed is good"—is thoroughly internalized by Gekko. In one poignant scene, Gekko summarizes to his gullible protégé Bud Fox, played by Charlie Sheen, the dynamic nature of the power elite in America:

> You've got 90 percent of the American public out there with little or no net worth. I create nothing, I own. We make the rules: the news, war, peace, famine, upheaval, the price of a paper clip. We pick that rabbit out of the hat while everybody sits out there and figures out how the hell we did it. Now, you're not naïve enough to think that we're living in a democracy?

While *Wall Street* examines the world of corporate greed, the 1988 film *Colors* is about a different aspect of crime in America. The tagline for this film is "70,000 gang members. One million guns. Two cops." Sean Penn and Robert Duvall play two police officers trying to combat gang violence as they patrol the streets of East Los Angeles.

Lawmakers have paid substantial attention to gang violence and street crime and inadequate attention to corporate crime. Perhaps this is because street crime is visible and corporate crime is not. While America has tolerated corporate crime, it has been harshly intolerant of street crime. Which poses the greatest harm to society?

In 2004, four Chinese corporate executives were executed for bank fraud involving $15 million. China sent a bold message to corporate criminals. In this case, there was no slap on the wrist, no federal pardons, no vacation at a Club Fed. Instead, the Chinese corporate crooks received capital punishment—an action reserved for the perpetrators of the most serious violent crimes in the U.S. Perhaps China saw defrauding investors of $15 million as a most serious violent crime.

References

Associated Press. 2005. Cops clearing city; White House: Barbara's comments "personal." *Chicago Tribune*, 8 September.

Dochat, Tom. 2004. Grass will serve his sentence in Florida. *The Patriot News* (Harrisburg, PA), 24 June.

Domhoff, G. William.1978. *The Powers That Be*. New York: Vintage Books.

Grant, Peter, and Christine Nuzum. 2004. Adelphia founder and one son are found guilty. *Wall Street Journal*, 9 July.

Hoelter, Herbert. 2002. The myth of "Club Fed." *Milwaukee Journal Sentinel*. 30 August.

Huffington, Arianna. 2003. *Pigs at the Trough*. New York: Crown Publishers.

James, George. 1995. Extra community service, U.S. tells Leona Helmsley. *New York Times*, 16 September.

Johnson, Carrie. 2005. Citigroup to settle with Enron investors. *Washington Post*, 11 June.

Kaplan, Peter. 2004. Feds: Cigarette makers lied for 50 years. Reuters Business, 21 September. Accessed at http://independent-media. tv/itemprint.cfm?fmedia_id=9063&fcategory_desc=Health.

Kirst, Sean. 2004. Nader charges Democrats turn blind eye to corporate power. Newhouse News Service, 28 July.

Kraft, Michael, and Scott Furlong. 2004. *Public Policy: Politics, Analysis, and Alternatives.* Washington, DC: CQ Press.

Lane, Charles. 2005. Justices toss out Enron over jury remarks. *Washington Post*, 1 June.

Locke, John. [1690] 1967. *Two Treatises on Government.* Cambridge: Cambridge University Press.

McGhee, Tom. 2003. Prison no picnic for former executives. *Denver Post.* 12 October.

Mills, C. Wright. 1959. *The Power Elite.* New York: Oxford University Press.

Mitchell, Russ. 2002. White-collar prison camp still hard time. *Houston Chronicle.* 18 August.

New York Times. 1997. U.S. judge approves 1980s insider settlements. 11 February.

New York Times. 2002. Steve Madden, shoe designer, begins his prison term. 21 September.

New York Times Magazine. 2004. Fraud's fallout. 6 June.

Norris, Floyd. 1998. Milken is gone, but junk still reigns. *New York Times*, 1 March.

PR News. 2004. Three blind mice: PR lessons from Enron, Global Crossing, and WorldCom. PR News 60, no. 13 (29 March). Accessed at http://www.prandmarketing.com/cgi/catalog/info?PRN.

Reckard, Scott E., and David Rosenzweig. 1999. Keating pleads guilty to fraud; Legal saga ends. *Los Angeles Times*, 17 April.

Reinman, Jeffrey. 1995. *The Rich Get Richer and the Poor Get Prison.* Boston: Allyn and Bacon.

Romero, Simon, and Jayna Desai. 2004. Satisfaction and sadness at sight of handcuffs. *New York Times*, 9 July.

Rushe, Dominic. 2003. When the law feels your white collar. *London Times*, 27 July.

Sachdev, Ameet. 2005. Schrushy acquitted on all charges. *Houston Chronicle*, 29 June.

San Francisco Chronicle. 1997. The Keating connections in the savings and loan scandal. 19 December.

Schlosser, Eric. 2002. *Fast Food Nation*. New York: Perennial.

Simon, David, and D. Stanley Eitzen. 1990. *Elite Deviance*. Boston: Allyn and Bacon.

Sloan, Allen. 2004. Lay's a victim? Not a chance. *Newsweek* 144, no. 3 (19 July).

The Economist. 2004. Leaders justice for bosses; corporate crime. *The Economist* 37, no. 8379.

Tyco Fraud Information Center. Accessed at http://www.tycofraudinfo center.com/information.php.

Winslow, George. 2003. Capital crimes. In *Prison Nation: The Warehousing of America's Poor*, edited by Tara Herivel and Paul Wright. New York: Routledge.

Chapter 8

The Prison Business

The **business** of prisons includes the positioning of prison guard unions as influential interest groups, the proliferation of prisons, and the role of prison labor in a cycle of capitalistic exploitation. Economically disadvantaged regions that lost manufacturing jobs in the 1970s and 1980s and were left out of the economic boom of the 1990s have come to rely on prisons as primary sources of employment. Big companies involved in the prison industry enjoy billions of dollars in income. Businesses also take advantage of cheap prison labor. This lowers their costs, increases their profits—and decreases the number of jobs available to the general population.

Corrections Officers Union

The corrections officers unions in each state seek to preserve their function in society. No corrections officers union has been as successful at this as the California Correctional Peace Officers Association (CCPOA). Unions in other states have attempted to mimic the strategies of the CCPOA in order to gain power and influence in their own state legislatures. The CCPOA remains the most powerful corrections officers union in the country. It serves as a model case study on effective interest-group politics.

I invited a sergeant from one of the California prisons to guest speak in my Master's in Public Administration class, Diversity and the Criminal Justice System. After his candid one-hour lecture, I asked, "Is the prison guard union, the CCPOA, as powerful as I have read?" He responded, "Uh-oh, uh-OH. You have no idea how powerful

CCPOA is. You have absolutely no idea!" The speaker's animated response led me to believe that the California Correctional Peace Officers Association wields an enormous amount of influence that is invisible to the public eye.

The CCPOA is the primary engineer behind California's hyperpunitive corrections policies. No other entity is responsible for constructing so many tough-on-crime policies. In fairness to the CCPOA, it is in their interest to advocate incarceration over drug treatment programs and punishment over rehabilitation. From their perspective, it makes sense to advocate for policies that maintain high recidivism rates rather than reducing them. They preserve their jobs and maintain an important function in society by incarcerating individuals. From a big-picture perspective, however, society is not benefiting from the staunchly tough policies of the CCPOA.

Judith Tannenbaum, author of *Disguised as a Poem: My Years Teaching Poetry at San Quentin*, has this to say about the union's motives and influence:

> The union's Political Action Committee Fund depends on members' dues, the sum of which depends on the total number of correctional officers contributing which, in turn, depends on the number of incarcerated men and women. Pay raises and perks are one thing. But it's something else again when the CCPOA lobbies to influence state laws and policy in ways that result in locking up more people. In the past 15 years, there's been a 400 percent increase in the number of people incarcerated. All the while, the [California] State Department of Corrections has resisted any attempt to open to public scrutiny what happens behind prison walls. (Tannenbaum 1999, A25)

CCPOA is the most influential interest group in California. How did this union evolve from being disorganized, underpaid, and underappreciated, to being the most powerful force in California politics? Prior to 1982, California state employees were not allowed to bargain collectively with their employers. They could only "meet and confer," which meant that although suggestions and employee complaints had to be heard, employees had no real leverage. Legal challenges to the State Employer-Employee Relations Act resulted in the passage of

Dill's Act in 1982. This gave all state employees the right to enter into collective bargaining units. As a consequence, several unions jockeyed to represent the prison guards. The name of the California Correctional Officers Association (CCOA) was changed to California Correctional Peace Officers Association when that union won the right to represent all the correctional officers statewide.

The prominence of CCPOA can be traced to the political savvy of one man in particular. Don Novey was elected CCOA president in 1980. To consolidate his base, Novey combined California Youth Authority supervisors, prison guards, and parole officers. Union membership increased from 6,000 to 31,000. Through aggressive employee recruitment, lobbying and cultivation of political alliances, the wise use of political action committees (PACs), and a large-scale public relations campaign, Novey transformed the CCPOA from what he describes as "a disorganized bunch of knuckle-draggers" into the most formidable force in California politics (Warren 2000, A1). Since 1990, the CCPOA has been among the top political donors in the state, giving Governor Pete Wilson $425,000 for his reelection campaign in 1994. This contribution was reported to be the largest single donation ever made to a candidate in California at that time (Tannenbaum 1999, A25).

In the organization's own words, the mission of the legal department of CCPOA is to:

- Provide high-quality legal representation to CCPOA's correctional peace officer members who are on the "front lines" of a difficult and dangerous profession;

- Aggressively address both violations of law and the Constitutional rights afforded to correctional peace officers;

- Support CCPOA's role as the exclusive representative for the California State Bargaining Unit 6 in areas of collective bargaining involving the terms and conditions of employment, including representation of CCPOA in arbitration disputes arising from the collective bargaining unit agreement;

- Zealously defend CCPOA's correctional peace officer members who stand accused of misconduct resulting from the challenges of working the toughest beat in the State; and,

- Further the larger mission of CCPOA: "to promote and improve the Correctional profession and to foster the welfare of those engaged in Corrections."

There are mission statements for various departments in the CCPOA, and the organization adheres to them all. The larger mission is insular in nature, with the interests of members given highest priority. This creates an organizational culture that is focused inward. Although the CCPOA manages public relations to remind the public of members' roles in securing their safety, the legal department's mission statement makes no mention of the public's best interests. Using words such as "aggressively" and "zealously" gives a clear understanding of the CCPOA's commitment to protecting its members above all else.

CCPOA has lobbied for the passage of tough-on-crime legislation and for the construction of more prison facilities. They are able to offer formidable opposition to anyone who advocates for humanistic corrections reform. The union has an annual operating budget of almost $20 million and employs twelve labor attorneys and five full-time lobbyists, plus a consulting public relations team. With the union collecting approximately $80 per month from each member and $75 from nonmembers, it has amassed the financial resources required to play—and win—the rugged game of politics.

In 1980, the average salary of prison guards was $14,440. By 2005 this had increased to about $55,000. In the midst of a state budget crisis in 2002, when a pay freeze was imposed on other state employees, CCPOA negotiated a significant raise for prison guards. Governor Gray Davis signed a five-year contract with the CCPOA, which the legislature approved. CCPOA contributed $1.1 million to Gray Davis's 2002 reelection campaign (Richman 2003, 1). In 2005, a 37 percent pay raise for the union took effect.

The CCPOA has formed coalitions with victims' rights organizations such as the Doris Tate Victims Bureau and Crime Victims United of California. This has increased the pressure to pass tough-on-crime legislation, including Proposition 187 in 1993, which established the three strikes law. CCPOA was the primary architect and the most influential supporter of this initiative. After proponents secured 800,000 signatures, the proposition was put on the ballot, received 72 percent approval, and became law.

Although violence occurs in less than 14 percent of all crimes, the CCPOA has done a remarkable job of inciting fear among California's residents. This has prompted the public to blindly endorse laws that are not in their best interest. Punishment-only corrections policies and high recidivism rates do not contribute positively to the public's well-being. Nevertheless, the public has been scared and hoodwinked into supporting policies endorsed by CCPOA. There is nothing democratic about this kind of political gamesmanship.

The Prison Economy

In the last 20 years the United States has built more prisons than any country during any period in history. The cost of the U.S. criminal justice system now runs $147 billion per year. But the financial costs are only part of the story. There are other costs not so easily seen, costs passed on to those least able to pay them—the poor rural towns in which most prisons are built and the poor urban communities from which most prisoners are sent. Because the costs of the current prison expansion are being passed to people of color, we say that prisons are examples of economic injustice and environmental racism. (Critical Resistance and California Moratorium Project 2005)

Prison construction is now a central part of the U.S. economy. During the past two decades, corporations and rural communities have become the primary beneficiaries of the incarceration boom. The prison economy has disproportionately exploited people of color. How can Americans who claim to be patriotic and nationalistic so carelessly exploit any sector of the American population in this way?

As U.S. jobs have become more technologically advanced and service-oriented, there has been a dramatic decline in jobs involving manufacturing, farming, mining, and timberwork. Rural areas that once depended on these types of jobs are struggling to deal with high unemployment and economic stagnation. The same communities that fought fiercely to keep prisons from being built in their areas two decades ago now fight just as fiercely to attract them. Some have attempted to increase their competitiveness by upgrading sewer and water systems and offering subsidized housing for prison employees. It is not uncommon for communities to invite prison representatives to town-hall meetings for presentations on the benefits of building a prison in their locality. Flyers and handouts are distributed in coffee shops highlighting the positive and stabilizing economic impact a "non-seasonal fluctuating" and "non-polluting" industry such as a prison facility would have on the local economy. Today, prisons are among the top three economic enterprises in rural communities, employing large numbers of people and providing reasonably good wages (Huling 2002, 1).

Corrections Corporation of America (CCA), the largest private prison corporation in the U.S., makes this claim on its Web site:

> Through CCA's ownership of correctional facilities, the company provides valuable economic benefits to its local community partners by paying property, sales and other taxes, and providing a stable employment base. CCA is a strong contributor in the communities in which our facilities are located, with a dedication to charitable giving and volunteerism. (Corrections Corporation of America 2005)

Crescent City, California, is a classic example of how a prison facility can transform a town. Home to the Pelican Bay State Prison, Crescent City in northern California is a town of a little more than 10,000 people. Pelican Bay has a payroll of more than $50 million and an annual budget of over $90 million. The prison employs about 1,500 people. In addition, the town holds the prison's hospital and garbage contracts. The economic activity stimulated by the prison lured K-Mart and Safeway to the area. Housing prices eventually doubled, bringing extra revenue to Crescent City from real estate taxes (Shelden 2004).

Not all civic transformations match that of Crescent City. There are limitations to what a prison facility can do for a local economy. For example, while it is true that prisons bring jobs to rural communities, local residents make up only 40 percent of those employed in the industry. The prison employment system is based on seniority, and the best paying jobs will go to those who have experience and education. Many rural residents possess neither the experience nor the educational background to rise to managerial positions.

Correctional officers unions and private developers are the primary lobbyists behind the astronomical increases in both incarceration rates and prison construction. These special-interest groups have energetically lobbied for three strikes laws, mandatory minimums, and other legislation requiring offenders to serve up to 80 percent of their time. An increase in the prison population translates into new jobs, higher wages, and government contracts. Each year, dozens of new prison facilities are built to house an ever-increasing prison population. In 1995 alone, 150 new prisons were built in the U.S. At an average cost of $105 million per prison, each new prison bed consumed approximately $57,000 of taxpayer money.

The American Legislative Exchange Council (ALEC) grew out of the emerging prison economy. This organization's ostensible operational strategy is to enlist state legislators from all parties and members of the private sector who share its mission. The purpose of ALEC is to engage in an ongoing effort to promote Jeffersonian principles among elected officials, the private sector, and the general public, for the purpose of enacting substantive and genuine legislative reforms consistent with the ALEC mission.

In practice, ALEC has been an enthusiastic advocate for the prison industry. It is made up of an array of diverse stakeholders, including state legislators, prison officials, corporate representatives, and criminal justice officials. A significant number of politicians belong to this group. In fact, ALEC membership will invariably be represented in legislative houses throughout the country. One of the major subcommittees within ALEC is the Criminal Justice Task Force, with its objective of constructing laws on crime and punishment. These laws will ultimately be beneficial to the group's members. Many of the companies who are members of ALEC have lucrative contracts with prisons. They take advantage of cheap prison labor. The Corrections Corporation of America is one member. CCA is joined by other like-minded corporations, including Ameritech, AT&T, Sprint, Pfizer, and Bayer. Each member pays annual dues ranging from $5,000 to $50,000. Corporations such as Exxon Mobil, Chevron, Proctor and Gamble, and Ford are exempt from paying dues because they contribute to ALEC financially via grants (Shelden 2004).

In analyzing who is profiting from the prison economy, Eve Goldberg and Linda Evans point out, "investment houses, construction companies, architects and support services such as food, medical, transportation and furniture, all stand to profit" along with "a burgeoning 'specialty item' industry sell[ing] fencing, handcuffs, drug detectors, protective vests, and other security devices to prisons" (Goldberg and Evans).

Hundreds of goods and services are required to operate a prison. Big corporations are increasingly competing for the opportunity to enter this profitable enterprise, with little sensitivity to the needs of the inmates and their families. For example, approximately 60 percent of prisons are built in rural areas, but 80 percent of inmates are from urban areas (Huling 2002). When prisons employ rural white corrections officers, with little experience in dealing with diverse populations, to monitor the behavior of minorities from the inner city, it creates a tense situation. Moreover, when inmates are incarcerated in rural areas far from their homes and communities, it is very difficult for families and friends to visit on a consistent basis. Familial support, in the context of prison visits, fosters positive attitudes among inmates. In many cases, visits are the only element keeping some inmates sane.

Federal law requires that every individual residing in a district be counted in the census. Although inmates do not get to vote, in the spirit of the Two-Thirds Compromise—which counted slaves as two-thirds of a person for the purposes of establishing legislative representation—areas with prison facilities get to count the number of inmates as a part of their overall population. This dynamic strengthens a district's representative influence. In addition, because prisoners make little or no wages, the per capita income in the area is lowered. As a consequence, towns are able to apply for state and federal poverty grants for which only low-income areas are eligible. According to *Wall Street Journal* reporter Nicholas Kulish, the town of Calipatria, California, used its poverty grant to improve city streets. In Ionia, Michigan, poverty grant funds were used to install laptop computers in town vehicles and transform the town's National Guard armory into a community center (Kulish 2001, 1).

Some industries actually prosper because of crime. In addition to the production of goods for the corrections industry, more prisons mean larger pools of low-cost labor. Although this sounds like a conspiratorial effort by the elites to benefit from the failings of minorities, this behavior is consistent with the ugly history of American capitalism. Whenever there is a clash between democracy and capitalism in the U.S., capitalism always wins. Whenever there is a clash between protecting human rights and promoting capitalism, capitalism always rules the day. There is no more highly held value among the elites in the U.S. than making a profit. What corporations have done with the maquiladora factories in the Free Trade Zones in Central America, they are now doing in the U.S. With a blatant disregard for human rights, American corporations scour the world looking for regions with the lowest wages, no unions, no safeguards for human or worker rights, no occupational safety or environmental standards, and no red tape. When these ideal conditions are met, they set up their factories. In the same spirit, U.S. corporations have turned their insensitive and inhumane practices loose on the home front, to exploit this country's disadvantaged citizens with the same fervor as they have exploited poor people around the world.

The toll that the prison economy is taking on minority communities is incalculable. The pain and suffering brought on by greed and hyper-capitalism translate directly into violations of human rights. The prison economy has entangled millions of people in a zero-sum game quagmire in which there are clear winners and losers. When the U.S. spends hundreds of billions of dollars on the war in Iraq, big business wins all the way around. They win with the lucrative contracts garnered from the war and they win at home. Given the costs of war, there is little left in the national budget to meet urgent domestic needs, such as substantive programs that deter kids from criminal activity. Over the years, there have been deep cuts to crime prevention programs. This only benefits those invested in the prison industry. Big corporations are increasingly profiting from ill-advised governmental policies.

Private Prisons

In Colorado, private companies operate more than 3,500 prison beds. This means that 20 percent of the state's prison capacity is managed by the private sector. Officials of private prison companies argue that privatization helps save financially strapped states while providing quality services. Other advocates maintain that privately run prisons help alleviate overcrowding because they are quicker to complete and cheaper to build. Private prisons can be constructed for 25 percent less than public facilities.

Critics, however, weigh the downside of privately run prisons against the benefits their supporters describe. A vicious riot at a southern Colorado facility in 2004 prompted state lawmakers to reevaluate the costs and benefits of private prisons. During the same period, a riot broke out at a facility in Watonga, Oklahoma. Hundreds of inmates wielding baseball bats, fire extinguishers, and two-by-fours terrorized each other and the guards (Kelly 2004).

There is a debate simmering throughout the U.S. regarding the merits of private prisons. Before 1983, it was the government's position that housing, monitoring, and in some cases, rehabilitating the incarcerated population was solely its responsibility. The U.S. government seemed to believe—accurately—that the serious business of incarceration and rehabilitation should not be left in private hands. Before 1983, governmental officials were convinced that only they were capable of protecting the interests of society and the constitutional and civil rights of those incarcerated. The magnitude and seriousness of this responsibility did not change in 1983, but the government's position did. The values and principles that were so tightly held before 1983 quickly evaporated with the founding in Nashville, Tennessee, of the Corrections Corporation of America. It is a classic case of hyper-capitalism undermining the U.S. government's role as a fair and compassionate leviathan that upholds constitutional principles and acts in the interests of the public.

CCA was the first private prison provider in the U.S. In 1983, the company entered into its first detention center contract by building and operating a facility for the Bureau of Citizenship and Immigration Services in Texas. CCA is now the largest private corrections system in the U.S and the sixth largest overall. The company ranks behind only the federal government and four state correctional systems in terms of numbers of beds and prisoners. CCA operates more than 50 percent of the beds in private prisons.

CCA contracts with federal, state, and local authorities to manage prison facilities and owns 38 of its own facilities. For those who need proof that the prison industry is big business, CCA stock is traded alongside Nike, Disney, McDonald's, and Coca-Cola. CCA joined the New York Stock Exchange in 1994 and bears the symbol CXW. The company manages some 67,000 beds in more than 60 facilities across 19 states, including the District of Columbia. Federal correctional and detention authorities account for some 35 percent of CCA sales, with a 95 percent contract renewal rate. The CCA Web site states that the company "offers a variety of rehabilitation and educational programs, including basic education, life skills and employment training and substance abuse treatment. The company also provides health care (including medical, dental and psychiatric services), food service and work and recreational programs" (Corrections Corporation of America 2005). For the transportation of inmates from location to location, CCA teams with TransCor America Unit, which provides services for over 2,000 correctional agencies nationwide (Woodruff 2005).

One of CCA's chief competitors is Cornell Companies, Inc. They are also traded on the New York Stock Exchange, under the symbol CRN. Cornell builds and operates community-based correctional centers. They manage more than 80 adult and juvenile facilities in 15 states, including Washington, DC. They are responsible for approximately 18,500 beds. On paper, the company provides job training and placement, recreation and leisure activities, health care (including mental health and drug counseling), and life skills training (Woodruff 2005).

The GEO Group, Inc., is another big corporation that is heavily invested in the prison business. GEO runs more than 40 correctional, detention, and mental health facilities throughout the U.S. Although this country is the company's primary market, they also operate facilities in Canada, Australia, New Zealand, and South Africa. GEO manages 35,300 beds. The U.S. government, California, Florida, and

New York Stock Exchange Fact Sheet:
Corrections Corporation of America

Company Type	Public (NYSE: CXW)
Fiscal Year-End	December
2004 Sales (in millions)	1,148.3
1-Year Sales Growth	10.4 percent
2004 Net Income (in millions)	62.5
1-Year Net Income Growth	55.9 percent
2004 Employees	15, 420
1-Year Employee Growth	11.7 percent

Source: Woodruff 2005.

New York Stock Exchange Fact Sheet:
Cornell Companies, Inc.

Company Type	Public (NYSE: CRN)
Fiscal Year-End	December
2004 Sales (in millions)	291.0
1-Year Sales Growth	7.1 percent
2004 Net Income (in millions)	7.4
1-Year Net Income Growth	54 percent
2004 Employees	4,192
1-Year Employee Growth	3.7 percent

Source: Woodruff 2005.

New York Stock Exchange Fact Sheet:
The GEO Group, Inc.

Company Type	Public (NYSE: GGI)
Fiscal Year-End	December
2004 Sales (in millions)	614.5
1-Year Sales Growth	0.5 percent
2004 Net Income (in millions)	16.8
1-Year Net Income Growth	62.9 percent
2004 Employees	4,192
1-Year Employee Growth	12.3 percent

Source: Woodruff 2005.

Texas are their major customers. Similar to other private prison companies, they offer—on paper—educational, rehabilitative, and vocational training programs at their facilities (Woodruff 2005).

Private companies are in the prison business to make money. Cost-cutting measures that have the potential to increase profits but put inmates and employees at risk are unwise. All major private prison companies state in their profiles that they offer educational, rehabilitative, and vocational training programs. If these programs are truly offered in each instance with the seriousness of the problems they are intended to eradicate, then this is indeed a good thing. However, from a purely logical perspective, one has to ask: What do private prison companies gain by rehabilitating inmates? Their capitalistic instincts cause them to be insensitive to the well-being of the broader society. From a Lockean perspective, private prison firms have not entered into—nor are they bound by—the same social contract with the people as the government. From the perspective of John Stuart Mills and utilitarianism, private prison firms, unlike the government, do not have a responsibility to adhere to policies that ensure the greatest good for the greatest number of people. Without the systematic monitoring of their behavior by the government—which does not now occur—the private prison industry will embrace generic formulas that maintain or increase their profit margins.

In a comprehensive series of articles about prison health care, *New York Times* reporter Paul von Zielbauer reveals the dire cost of privatizing health care for inmates. Many private prisons contract with for-profit health service companies. These now account for approximately 40 percent of all inmate medical care. Over the past decade, Prison Health Services, Correctional Medical Services, and other profit-making companies have won prison contracts worth hundreds of millions of dollars. The Prison Health Services marketing pitch is: "Take the messy and expensive job of providing medical care from overmatched government officials, and give it to an experienced nationwide outfit that could recruit doctors, battle lawsuits, and keep costs down" (2005, 1.1).

Regardless of its enticing sales pitch, Prison Health Services does not have any strong incentive to improve the health or the quality of life of the inmates they are contracted to serve. A year-long study conducted by *The New York Times* revealed the actual practices and procedures of Prison Health Services. The company has paid million of dollars in fines and settlements. The study found:

> ... repeated instances of medical care that has been flawed and sometimes lethal. The company's performance around the nation has provoked criticism from judges and sheriffs, lawsuits from inmates' families and whistle-blowers, and condemnations by federal, state and local authorities.... In the two deaths [and eight others] across upstate New York, state investigators say they kept discovering the same failings: medical staffs trimmed to the bone, doctors under-qualified or out of reach, nurses doing tasks beyond their training, prescription drugs withheld, patient records unread and employee misconduct. (von Zielbauer 2005, 1.1)

The problems that plague Prison Health Services are emblematic of the risks of privatizing prisons. Each company in the industry offers to produce services at lower and lower costs. The ferocious competitive process compels companies to put in unreasonably low bids. After they secure the contract, they figure out ways to cut costs and recoup the line items given up during the bidding process. As Dr. Michael Puisis, the editor of *Clinical Practice in Correctional Medicine*, states:

> It's almost a game of attrition, where the companies will take bids for amounts that you just can't do it for. Businesses with the most dubious track records can survive, and thrive. When cost-trimming cuts into the quality of care, harming inmates and prompting lawsuits and investigations, governments often see no alternatives but to keep the company, or hire another, then another when that one fails—a revolving-door process that sometimes ends with governments rehiring the company they fired years earlier. (von Zielbaur 2005, 5)

If companies such as the Corrections Corporation of America were as serious as they state about meeting their rehabilitation objectives, they would hire well-trained and well-educated prison guards and social workers. They would recruit the best psychiatrists, psychologists, and doctors for their facilities. But they do not hire these types of professionals. Why? Because it would cut into their $1.1 billion in sales and their $62 million in annual profits. In other words, it does not make economic sense for private companies to enthusiastically embrace rehabilitation. Hence, it does not make sense for the government entities who contract with private providers to believe that these enterprises are altruistic by nature. Rehabilitation reduces recidivism. Low recidivism rates are in the best interests of society. Private firms do not have an incentive to lower recidivism rates. They, theoretically, have no interest in doing what is best for society. In an effort to deal with the burgeoning prison population of the 1980s and 1990s, various stakeholders bought the counterintuitive rhetoric of private prison firms. It has proven to be nothing more than window dressing.

Corporations Inside Prisons

No industry is more symbolic of the exploitative practices of corporations doing business inside prison walls than telephone companies. Inmates are not allowed to use calling cards. This is peculiar, since a calling card would not appear on the surface to be dangerous contraband. If inmates used them, prison authorities could still monitor their calls. Instead, inmates must make collect telephone calls. My mentally ill cousin has been incarcerated on numerous occasions. Each time he would call me collect from his detention facility. I was appalled at the charges—as much as $40 for a 10-minute call. Very few families can afford to pay these astronomical telephone fees. Hence, they block their phones so the inmates' calls are not put through. In many cases, all an inmate has to look forward to during his grueling week is a 10-minute phone call with loved ones. These calls keep many inmates buoyant and sane. When families can no longer take their calls, it is psychologically devastating to the inmates and to the families. My parents had to put a block on their phone because of calls coming in from my cousin. They made a gallant effort; but paying an extra $200 per month for a few 10-minute conversations eventually took its toll on their budget.

Telephone companies contract with prisons to take 50 percent of the profit on phone calls. The prison takes the other 50 percent. The prisons inflate the prices of calls to 30 to 50 percent of the market rate. This means that a one-minute, long-distance call could cost between $3 and $5. Each prison telephone used by inmates can yield up to $12,000 per year. There are phones peppered throughout prison yards, and inmates are always eager to use them. Inmates make over $1 billion in phone calls per year (Hallinan 2001, xiv). Thus some prisons make hundreds of thousands of dollars in revenue each year. This is a predatory practice that has an incalculable impact on inmates and their families. It is as vicious as some of the crimes committed by those in prison.

The use of cheap inmate labor by corporations is also a source for concern. Increasingly this is becoming a controversial issue. There are, to be sure, concrete benefits to be derived from prison labor. According to prison officials, inmates who work are 24 percent less likely to commit crimes and 14 percent more likely to be employed in the twelve years after they are released from incarceration, compared with inmates who do not participate in work programs. However, inmates who work for corporations inside prisons only receive a fraction of their pay. In many cases, inmates are required to pay restitution to their victims and contribute to a general crime victims' fund. Sometimes inmates are required to pay room and board and reimburse the state for other costs of their own incarceration.

In federal and state prisons, 80 percent of inmates work at some point during their incarceration. The majority of these jobs involve maintaining the institution. This type of prison labor is non-controversial and has always been accepted. However, using prison labor for corporations is now at the center of a heated national debate. The Washington State Supreme Court weighed in on the issue in 2004. In a 5-4 decision, the court ruled that it was unconstitutional to sell, essentially, inmate labor to private businesses operating inside prison walls. The state department of corrections announced that this decision would cost them $600,000 in room-and-board payments from inmates. The state's crime victims' fund would lose $150,000 in income. In its decision the court adhered to Article II, subsection 29 of the state constitution: "After the first day of January eighteen hundred and ninety, the labor of convicts of this state shall not be let out by contract to any person, co-partnership, company or corporation." Proponents of corporate prison labor, however, point to the portion of subsection 29 that reads, "and the Legislature shall by law provide for the working of convicts for the benefit of the state"(Ammons 2005, C3; Stephens 2003, B2).

In Massachusetts, ten prisons have shops where inmates produce items such as clothes, flags, and license plates. Prison authorities there are likely to use the latter part of Washington State's subsection 29 to defend their practices. Massachusetts Correctional Industries, known as MassCor, is a division of the state's Department of Corrections. MassCor has embraced the slogan "We're here for you ... ALWAYS." This slogan means that when inmates—working for $1 per hour—reupholster furniture, assemble mattresses, and make license plates, they are ultimately benefiting the people of Massachusetts. Half of the inmate's wages go into a savings account from which the state can be reimbursed for costs of the inmate's incarceration. The other half is put into another account from which the inmate can draw funds to buy items such as snacks, cosmetics, and clothes from the prison canteen. Inmates are not allowed to have cash on the prison yard (Sweeney 2004, 1).

The majority of MassCor items are sold to state and municipal agencies. However, anyone can order from the company's catalog. Twelve pairs of boxer shorts sell for $19.90, for example. The Massachusetts Department of Corrections sees only the benefits of prison labor. It gives many inmates who have never had a real job some legitimate work experience. It also gives them a chance to break the monotony of prison life. *Boston Globe* writer Emily Sweeney reports on an inmate worker named Kevin who states, "This is one of the best jobs I've had. For me it keeps me sane. I'm doing something." He continues, "Being idle is not something that's good for me." Inmates and the Department of Corrections see the prison work experience as a win-win scenario (2004, 1). There are others, however, who are not so enthusiastic about corporations using prison labor. The most vocal critics are the corporations that are not in the prisons. Their argument against the use of prison labor by other corporations is not that it exploits prisoners, per se; but rather that it gives some companies an unfair competitive advantage. In other words, there is absolutely no concern for the inmate in their argument.

The practices of Unicor, also known as Federal Prisons Industries, Inc. (FPI), are emblematic of the problems stemming from corporations using prison labor. Between 2000 and 2002, U.S. furniture makers were dramatically hurt by a 28 percent decrease in sales that amounted to $4.1 billion. Tens of thousands of workers were laid off. Sales of Unicor office furniture, however, increased almost 30 percent during the same period. Two distinct advantages drove the jump in Unicor's sales. "Inmates that work for Unicor make between 23 cents and $1.15 per hour. It is mandatory that all federal agencies purchase their furniture from Unicor, which is operated by the Federal Bureau of Prisons" (Kaiser 2004, 1). In other words, Unicor enjoys cheap labor costs and exclusive federal contracts.

Buyers and competitors in the business say that Unicor's monopoly is particularly problematic because they charge high prices and offer low quality. The Federal Bureau of Prisons defends Unicor's practices, stating that the company needs more work in order to help rehabilitate inmates. With sales reaching $700 million and products ranging from furniture to mattresses plus operating call centers, "businesses complain FPI abuses its near-monopoly powers over federal contracts by charging more than market prices and going so far as buying products from private companies, marking them up and reselling them to the government, costing taxpayers money without benefiting prisoners" (Kaiser 2004, 1). The U.S. would be quick to condemn these kinds of practices in other nations. We would criticize other countries for engaging in government-sanctioned corruption. We would withhold aid and force them to right their wrongs. But U.S. federal agencies are among the biggest consumers of prison labor. Inmates provide goods and services to the Environmental Protection Agency, Fish and Wildlife Services, the Coast Guard, the Department of Health and Human Services, and the Department of Transportation.

Corporations who stood on the sidelines for years complaining about unfair competitive advantages have now joined the fray. No longer taking the high road, they have campaigned vigorously and successfully to contract with prisons to use inmate labor. These companies include Boeing, Chevron, IBM, Dell, Honeywell, Microsoft, Motorola, and Eddie Bauer. TWA uses inmates to take airline reservations. Inmates stock shelves for Toys-R-Us and make uniforms for McDonald's. Victoria's Secret even uses inmate labor. Many other companies also find it advantageous to use cheap inmate labor (Quek 1999; Tech News 2001).

"Outsourcing" refers to the burgeoning practice by U.S. corporations of shipping jobs overseas to take advantage of lower labor costs. The new business practice of using cheap prison labor in the U.S. will likely fuel the controversial trend I call "inmate-sourcing." With a substantial number of jobs being shipped overseas, many jobs being placed inside prisons, and still others being taken by legal and illegal immigrants, how can the average person with little education and work experience expect to find decent employment? How is this situation patriotic? How does it mesh with the slogans and rhetoric embodied by America the Beautiful, The Greatest Nation on Earth, The American Dream, and chants of USA, USA, USA? And—as a side note—why would God continue to bless an America that embraces so many foul practices?

A New York State Department of Labor study found that 83 percent of those who violated their probation or parole were unemployed at the time of the violation (Atkinson 2002, 3). As Georgia parolee Fred Steed said, "Employment is King." President Bush's 2004 immigrant work proposal recommends giving two-year work permits to illegal immigrants, renewable indefinitely. Where is the President's comprehensive plan to find jobs for American citizens who have been incarcerated? Is it too idealistic to think that the billions of dollars used to house local, state, and federal inmates could be used in more creative and productive ways that are also more beneficial to society?

It is ironic that prisoners have a better chance of working at a job in prison than they do finding one on the outside. It is also a sad irony that the corporations for which inmates work so diligently are unlikely to hire those same inmates once they are released. It would be noble of corporations that make use of prison labor to develop systems to cultivate, mentor, and provide jobs for inmates when they complete their prison time.

Perhaps this is too much to ask of corporations who have saved millions of dollars by using inmate labor. Maybe this is an unrealistic expectation of corporations that have enthusiastically taken the low road. If prisoners cannot find gainful employment after they are released, despite their work experience on the inside, then the beneficial work experience touted by the Massachusetts Department of Corrections and others is inconsequential. What does it mean if inmates with work experience on the inside cannot find employment on the outside? It means that corrections departments and corporations have both been playing the cruel game of "Let's Exploit Them"—to the hilt.

References

American Legislative Exchange Council (ALEC). Mission statement. Accessed 10 June 2005 at http://www.alec.org/.

Ammons, David. 2005. Legislature: Return of prison labor program sought. *Columbian* (Vancouver, WA), 3 March.

Atkinson, Robert D. 2002. *Prison Labor: It's More Than Breaking Rocks.* Progressive Policy Institute. Accessed 13 June 2005 at http://www.ppionline.org.

California Correctional Peace Officers Association (CCPOA). History. Mission Statement. Accessed 10 June 2005 at http://www.ccpoa net.org/departments/Legal/mission.php.

Corrections Corporation of America. 2005. About CCA: CCA at a glance. Accessed 11 June 2005 at http://www.correctionscorp.com/aboutcca.html.

Critical Resistance and California Moratorium Project. 2005. *Prisons: New Forms of Environmental Racism.* Pamphlet.

Goldberg, Eve and Linda Evans. N.d. The prison industrial complex and the global economy. Accessed 22 May 2005 at http://www.prisonactivist.org/crisis/evans-goldberg.html.

Hallinan, Joseph T. 2001. *Going up River: Travels in a Prison Nation.* New York: Random House.

Huling, Tracy. 2002. Building a prison economy in rural America. Accessed at http://www.prisonsucks.com/scans/building.html.

Kaiser, Rob. 2004. Prison labor is cheap, tough for companies to beat. *Chicago Tribune,* 18 July.

Kelly, Sean. 2004. Riot reignites debate over private prisons, some say savings not worth the risks. *Denver Post,* 22 July.

Kulish, Nicholas. 2001. Annexing the penitentiary. *Wall Street Journal.* Accessed 22 May 2005 at http://www.grassrootsleadership.org/Articles/articles5_spr2002.html.

Quek, Samuel. 1999. Lockhart Prison locks down labor force. *The Working Stiff Journal* 2, no. 2. Reprinted in *The Daily Texan* and accessed 9 June 2005 at http://uts.cc.utexas.edu/~rjensen/vol2 no2/prison.htm.

Richman, Josh. 2003. Prison guards, state in dark on wage logistics. *Oakland Tribune,* 5 July.

Shelden, Randall. 2004. It's more profitable to treat the disease than to prevent it. Paper presented at the Justice Studies Association

Conference, Madison, WI. June. Accessed 22 May 2005 at http://www.sheldensays.com/Res-four.htm.

Stephens, Richard. 2003. Court hears arguments for, against prison labor. *Spokesman-Review* (Spokane, WA), 29 October.

Sweeney, Emily. 2004. Keeping busy behind bars: Inmates produce clothes, flags, license plates. *Boston Globe*, 19 February.

Tannenbaum, Judith. 1999. Prisons, a growth industry: Correctional officers union keeping it that way. *San Francisco Chronicle*, 27 September.

Tech News. 2001. Prison labor cheats society. 66, no. 8 (27 March). Accessed 8 June 2005 at http://www.wpi.edu/News/TechNews/010327/prisonlabor.shtml.

von Zielbauer, Paul, with Joseph Plambeck. 2005. As health care in jails goes private, 10 days can be a death sentence. *New York Times*, 27 February.

Warren, Jenifer. 2000. When he speaks, they listen. *Los Angeles Times*, 21 August.

Woodruff, David. 2005. Corrections Corporation of America, NYSE: CXW. *Hoover's New York Stock Exchange Overview*.

Appendix A

Perceptions of Criminal Justice Policies

For this book, I surveyed, with the help of student assistants, 500 residents of Southern California to get their opinions about criminal justice policies.

Question 1: Do you think there is racial bias in the criminal justice system?

African American

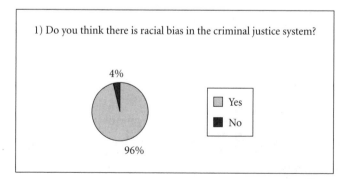

1) Do you think there is racial bias in the criminal justice system?

4%

96%

Yes
No

Response	Frequency	Percentage
Yes	52	96
No	3	4
Total	55	100

White

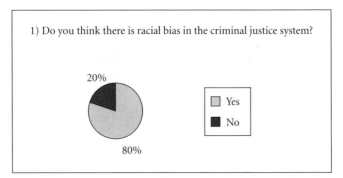

Response	Frequency	Percentage
Yes	97	80
No	25	20
Total	122	100

Latino

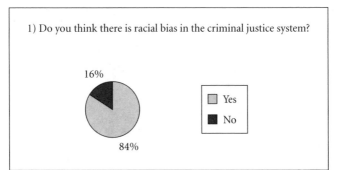

Response	Frequency	Percentage
Yes	102	84
No	20	16
Total	122	100

Asian

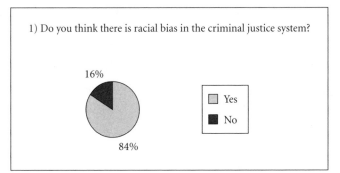

1) Do you think there is racial bias in the criminal justice system?

16%

84%

Yes
No

Response	Frequency	Percentage
Yes	127	84
No	25	16
Total	152	100

Other

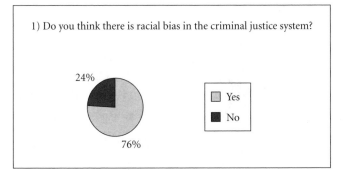

1) Do you think there is racial bias in the criminal justice system?

24%

76%

Yes
No

Response	Frequency	Percentage
Yes	37	76
No	12	24
Total	49	100

Question 2: Should rehabilitation opportunities be provided for inmates?

African American

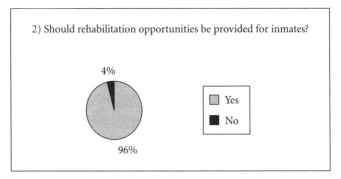

Response	Frequency	Percentage
Yes	52	96
No	3	4
Total	55	100

White

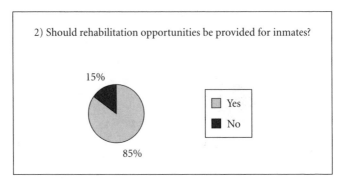

Response	Frequency	Percentage
Yes	105	85
No	17	15
Total	122	100

Latino

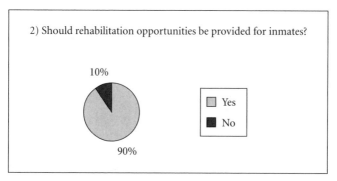

2) Should rehabilitation opportunities be provided for inmates?

Response	Frequency	Percentage
Yes	108	90
No	12	10
Total	120	100

Asian

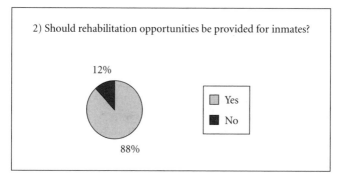

2) Should rehabilitation opportunities be provided for inmates?

Response	Frequency	Percentage
Yes	136	88
No	18	12
Total	154	100

Other

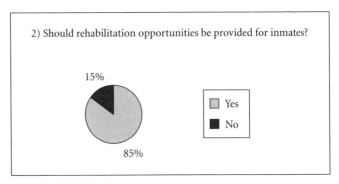

Response	Frequency	Percentage
Yes	42	85
No	7	15
Total	49	100

Question 3: Should parolees be provided job opportunities when they are released?

African American

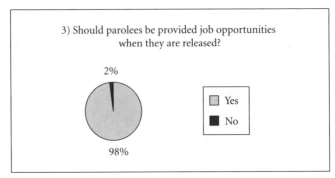

Response	Frequency	Percentage
Yes	54	98
No	1	2
Total	55	100

White

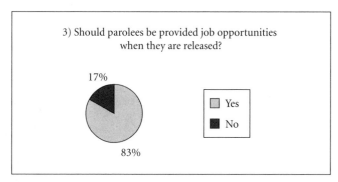

3) Should parolees be provided job opportunities when they are released?

17%

83%

Yes
No

Response	Frequency	Percentage
Yes	100	83
No	21	17
Total	121	100

Latino

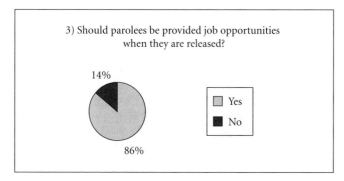

3) Should parolees be provided job opportunities when they are released?

14%

86%

Yes
No

Response	Frequency	Percentage
Yes	104	86
No	17	14
Total	121	100

Asian

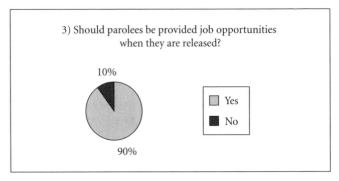

Response	Frequency	Percentage
Yes	139	90
No	15	10
Total	154	100

Other

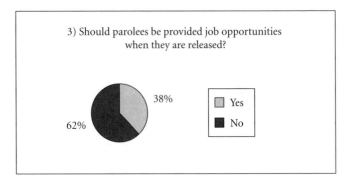

Response	Frequency	Percentage
Yes	20	38
No	32	62
Total	52	100

Question 4: In some states, there is a mandatory minimum sentence of 20 years to life for drug offenses. Do you think this type of sentencing is fair?

African American

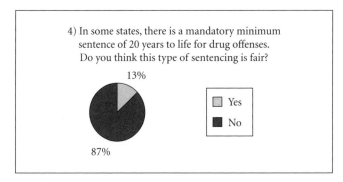

Response	Frequency	Percentage
Yes	7	13
No	47	87
Total	54	100

White

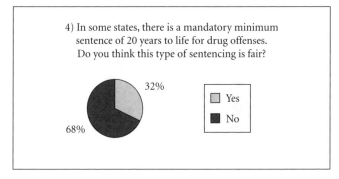

Response	Frequency	Percentage
Yes	38	32
No	82	68
Total	120	100

Latino

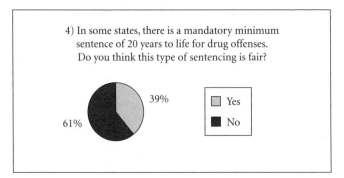

Response	Frequency	Percentage
Yes	47	39
No	74	61
Total	121	100

Asian

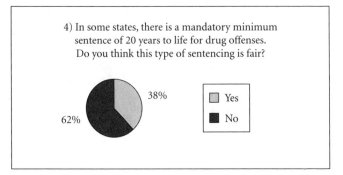

Response	Frequency	Percentage
Yes	58	38
No	95	62
Total	153	100

Other

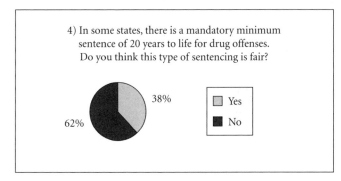

4) In some states, there is a mandatory minimum sentence of 20 years to life for drug offenses. Do you think this type of sentencing is fair?

38%
62%

☐ Yes
■ No

Response	Frequency	Percentage
Yes	20	38
No	32	62
Total	52	100

Question 5: Should drug-offending parolees have access to college financial aid and public assistance?

African American

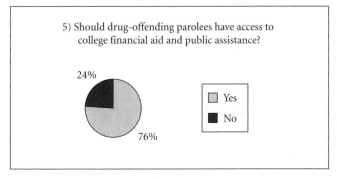

5) Should drug-offending parolees have access to college financial aid and public assistance?

24%
76%

☐ Yes
■ No

Response	Frequency	Percentage
Yes	42	76
No	13	24
Total	55	100

White

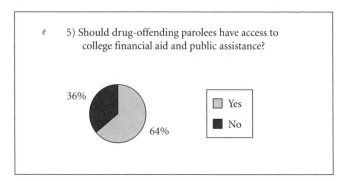

5) Should drug-offending parolees have access to college financial aid and public assistance?

36%   64%

Yes
No

Response	Frequency	Percentage
Yes	77	64
No	43	36
Total	120	100

Latino

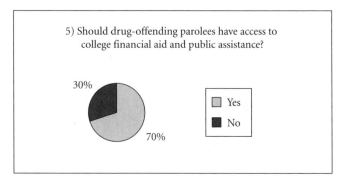

5) Should drug-offending parolees have access to college financial aid and public assistance?

30%   70%

Yes
No

Response	Frequency	Percentage
Yes	83	70
No	35	30
Total	118	100

Asian

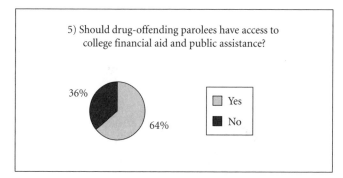

Response	Frequency	Percentage
Yes	99	64
No	55	36
Total	154	100

Other

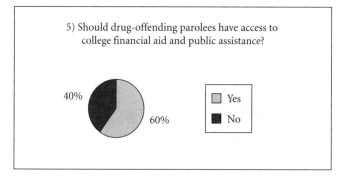

Response	Frequency	Percentage
Yes	32	60
No	21	40
Total	53	100

Question 6: Should parolees have the right to vote?

African American

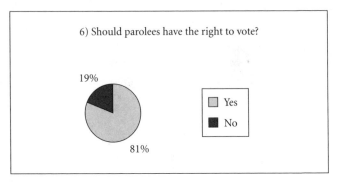

Response	Frequency	Percentage
Yes	46	81
No	9	19
Total	55	100

White

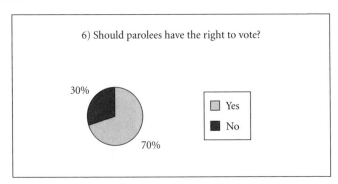

Response	Frequency	Percentage
Yes	84	70
No	36	30
Total	120	100

Latino

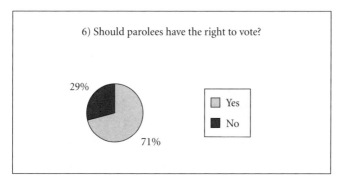

Response	Frequency	Percentage
Yes	87	71
No	35	29
Total	122	100

Asian

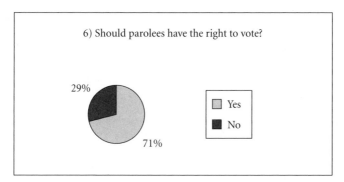

Response	Frequency	Percentage
Yes	109	71
No	44	29
Total	153	100

Other

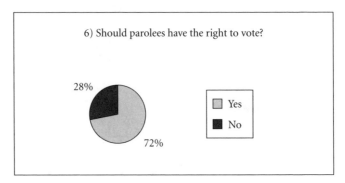

Response	Frequency	Percentage
Yes	36	72
No	14	28
Total	50	100

Appendix B

Reintegration Academy
Cal Poly Pomona

Renford Reese, Ph.D., and Micki Bryant, Ph.D.

The Reintegration Academy is a new program proposed at Cal Poly Pomona. It is designed to give juvenile ex-offenders the skills and support they need to reintegrate successfully into society.

Need for the Program

Education and the long-term economic opportunities and social benefits it creates are potent forces to reduce recidivism and prevent a return to gang affiliation and youth violence. A recent report on Reentry and the California Youth Authority found that wards of the California Youth Authority who participated in a postsecondary program demonstrated a recidivism rate that was significantly lower than the general juvenile ex-offender population. As many as 80 percent of those who participated in a college-level program did not return to prison. Reentry experts have clearly identified attending school and/or maintaining employment as major components of an individual's success in avoiding further incarceration. Parolees of various ages in California with at least two years of college have only a 10 percent rate of re-arrest, and a much higher rate of employment than those with no college education.

A majority of young offenders have experienced the detrimental effects of poverty, racism, and a lack of significant, positive social supports. Issues of mental health, substance abuse, and family dysfunction are also common among this population. When young offenders are released, they most often return to situations and communities where these conditions and issues have not changed. Gang affiliation is extremely high among youthful ex-offenders, and such affiliations are often strengthened during commitment due to the need for self-protection while incarcerated. Without encouragement and strategies to improve their chances for economic and social success, juvenile ex-offenders have little or no opportunity to make meaningful life changes.

In a national study of youth workforce development sponsored by the Annie E. Casey Foundation, education is identified as "the gateway to economic self-sufficiency." Meaningful employment correlates significantly with less delinquent and violent behavior among youth. Such employment must not merely be temporary make-work; it must lead to long-term career achievement. And while education can best prepare youth for sustained economic self-sufficiency, academic achievement must be accompanied by attainment of specific job skills and soft skills such as appropriate interpersonal and workplace behaviors. Some ex-offenders are able to function at the college level, although many require adequate support for academic remediation.

Program Description

The proposed Reintegration Academy will provide ex-offenders with an introduction to higher education that embraces academic, personal, and life skills development as well as career planning. Ten to fifteen participants will attend each ten-week session that parallels the academic quarter. The participants will range from 18 to 25 years of age. They will be referred by local organizations that work with ex-offenders, in conjunction with parole officers and case workers. Selection criteria will be used to screen prospective participants. Eligible ex-offenders will be those who, at a minimum, have a high school diploma or GED; are non-violent and non-sex offenders; demonstrate positive motivation for school; and have good character references from the referring organizations or parole officers.

For four hours each week, participants will engage in two main program components, **developmental activities** and **career planning**.

Developmental Activities

Two to three hours each week will be devoted to activities organized around four training modules designed to address personal, life skills, academic, and career development. Under faculty supervision, student interns will orchestrate some of the weekly activities and provide one-on-one peer support to participants. Other activities will be led by faculty.

The four training modules are:

- **Personal Development Module:** Ethics/Character Development, Anger/Stress Management, and Social Responsibility/Discipline Enrichment.

- **Life Skills Development Module:** Financial Planning, Organization and Time Management, and Wellness Issues/Concerns.

- **Academic Development Module:** Assessment of Academic Strengths and Weaknesses, Remediation Plan for Skill Area Deficits, and Introduction to Skills Needed at College Level; e.g., critical thinking.

- **Career Development Module:** Résumé Building, Communications Skills and Strategies, Technology Training.

An integrated approach is to be taken as participants are led through these modules. For example, they will be asked to produce short personal essays on subjects designed to start them thinking about goals and evaluating past behaviors. Topics might include reflections on their personal history and what influences led them to where they are today; why they want an education and how it fits with their goals; what needs to change in their lives so they can achieve those goals; and techniques for envisioning their lives five, ten, and fifteen years into the future. These papers will be used to improve writing skills as well as address themes such as ethics and personal character; communications; organization and planning; critical thinking; and academic achievement.

Each participant will be given an academic skills readiness screening, followed by guidance in pursuing any academic remediation that may be required. Some skills development will be incorporated into program activities; individuals who need more intensive remediation will be referred to appropriate resources. All participants will be instructed in basic computer skills, Internet use, library research, and job-search strategies. They will also receive assistance in developing a résumé and acquiring interview skills. Group activities and discussions will allow for the practice of interpersonal and communications skills. They will also foster ethics and character development, and propose personal strategies for conflict resolution, anger management, values identification, multicultural diversity, and problem-solving.

Career Planning

For several hours each week, professors and practitioners will provide introductory lectures and presentations about specific, tangible career opportunities. Participants will engage in some hands-on activities connected to particular fields of study offered on campus and explore career fields including:

- **Hotel and Restaurant Management**: Introducing areas such as Restaurant and Hotel Management, Quick Food Service Management, Catering and Banquet Management, and Professional Culinary Arts.

- **Arts and Music**: Introducing areas such as Acting, Film and American Culture, Painting, Printmaking and Graphic Design, and Music Business and Production.

- **Business and Agribusiness**: Introducing areas such as Entrepreneurial Strategies, Marketing, Management and Human Resources, Apparel Merchandising and Management, E-Commerce, Agriculture Skills and Facilities, Food Marketing and Agribusiness, and Food Science and Technology.

- **Kinesiology and Health Promotion:** Introducing areas such as Health Education and Promotion, Exercise Science, and Sports Medicine.

- **Environmental Design:** Introducing areas such as Landscape Architecture, Urban and Regional Planning, and Architecture.

Participants will sit in on classes and observe, for example, planning and food preparation for a working restaurant on campus. Their interests will be incorporated into their writing assignments, group discussions, academic planning, and career strategies. At the end of the ten-week session, they will participate in individual career-interest inventories sponsored by the campus Career Center. This will help guide them as they establish their personal academic and career goals.

Finally, each participant will make a concluding presentation that will allow them to showcase the skills they have acquired and share their successes and plans with the group.

*Thanks to Dr. Malia Lawrence for her contributions to the conceptual framework of the Reintegration Academy.

Appendix C

Poetic Injustice

Writing is a therapeutic exercise for many prison inmates, and more than a few are gifted writers. In their works they fuse their harsh realities and their dreams with enthusiasm and creativity.

When I met with inmates prior to writing this book, I told them I was holding a writing contest and the best entries would be published in *Prison Race*. My only requirement was that they write about their personal experiences with the prison system.

Inmates responded with poetry that is both real and true to their own lives and emotions.

Truth Of Consequences
by
Frederick Steed (aka, The Messenger)
Parolee, Georgia State Prison

Lock me down, take away my parole, do what you must do, but the truth must be told.

Put a number on me and mark me like a beast, while you all sit back, get rich and partake of your copious feast.

Pharaoh attempted to kill every male child and now this government has copped that same vicious style.

Reagan and Bush contaminated this Blessed Land, now they want to put their blame on every black man. They claim they want to help our innocent and misguided kids but how can they? When their parents are all doing mandatory bids.

For the harvest of the Earth is getting ripe and a lot of you real crooks are going to wear stripes. Stripes that God will mark on your backs, so he'll know how to keep your male factors intact, our kids are suffering and not for lottery funds. Our kids need their parents and that close-knit bond. Bureaucratic Manipulators are screaming "Get Tough on Crime" but what it boils down to is robbing the taxpayers for their last nickel and dime.

We need to open our eyes and see the real thief, for he holds the title of Governor, House Speaker, and Correctional Chief.

We have to go to the Bible/Koran and get a better understanding of God's will and search until we are able to reveal what God has sealed. You do your part and I'll do mine, and I'll meet each of you on the "battle front line."

The history is theirs but the future is ours.

Soul Freezs
by
William Fields (aka, Trey Devil)
Inmate #T51053, Centinela State Prison, California

Dark drips stream down my cheek and run down to the floor,

To occupy my space, mind, and soul who knows

where my thoughts flow when out of control.

Pause.

Wait for me, for here is where I stay in this cold perdition,

Clutching the inner depths of my decrepit soul with all
my strength.

A tenth of my life is gone—so much pain with little gain,

Stains of sweat soak my sheets no socks on my cold feet.

I hope you hear it palpitate when you're in a blissful sleep.

It's cold in my cell, but no one to tell and echoes of
colder yells.

Sleep, I try, even though I fail,

Cold buttons on the telephone, no one's ever home.

Cold water on my face [splash splash splash] embraces
me for another cold cold day.

Confined
by
Allen Williams
Inmate #810470, Calhoun State Prison, Georgia

As I sit here in an eight by twelve cell

Confined behind these walls, which is like living in hell

I'm left to drown in my sorrow, with my tears clutching
my face

Contemplating the actions that can't be erased

I was a man doing whatever it took to succeed

So blinded by sins and greed, til I'm no longer free

Who Am I?
by
Rufus Williams
Inmate #148015,
Chippewa Correctional Facility, Michigan

Tell me! Where am I at this young age? I'm locked in a cage like an animal in a rage. Am I crazy or mad? There's a difference—both are sad. The screams that echo from a prison cell bring up the reality of this man made hell.

I was labeled as a menace to society because I can't face sobriety.

Sobriety brings reality, and reality brings pain. My pain can't be handled by any human brain. My brain is criminally insane.

Nobody cares so I have nothing to share—dreams of death as I take my last breath. Where is my Savior? His lights, his grace? I must not be worthy—what a faceless disgrace. Where is the love? It went away long ago. Where it went I don't know. I ran out of luck so I don't give a fuck. Where will I be in my old age? Will I be locked in a cage like an animal in a rage?

PURPOSELY
by
Fundi
Inmate #D-87335, Centinela State Prison, California

Some of you folks may think I'm nice,

Others might test my cool

Then some will say that I've lost my way

And regard me as a fool

I'm a Black-Man

A product of this land,

And my place has been set aside

To dwell in hell in this prison cell

On this clandestine slavery ride

First and foremost, I must admit

My life began thru abuse

Directed towards crime

And there was no sign to guide me from misuse

Thru days and nights, I had to fight

To control the beast within,

And like the thoughts of many un-caught,

I acted out my sins

Alone again with nothing but men

In this cocoon that's self created,

This darker side is no where to hide,

But that can be debated

The divide and split

Of this slavery ship will keep us on this page,

We're segregated, and always hated

In a perpetual controlling stage

Deep in this darkness

Of this encapsulated soul,

Striving to be seen, heard

In a place that's so cold

Lost in an ambience

Of metal so unclear,

In a sea of exasperating noises

That I am forced to hear

Vicious stares of the angry men lost

Hopeless, soiled by the Earth

Suffering on a grand scale is what it all cost

The beauty of it all is that the feelings are more intense

And the slipping away is when you realize

That you are trapped in the middle of the desert,

Caged behind an electric, and barbed wired fence

Many believe that it is on the person,

And his purpose within

Some trip, fall, stumble, and perish

Just looking for a friend

The lost must believe that they can make a difference,

That they can reach their peak,

That they can shine like real gold,

When times are very bleak

Enter the Apex

And shine our light upon the young

Giving up straight game

And prove to them that there's nothing right with being wrong

So if you are amongst a chosen few

And you can grasp these seeds,

Then plant them in a fertile land,

And watch them meet our needs

And for those whom are lost, but enlightened

It is plain to see

The criminal justice system is a slave ship

To both you and me. So, stay FREE PURPOSELY!

Plant My Soul
by
Patrick "Top" Osborne
Inmate #V23607, Centinela State Prison, California

Ice Cold

Solid Ground

Rain

Rain

Earth Bound

Melted Heart

Wicked Start

Death Rise

Cried Out Eyes

Open Ground

Silence All Around

Eyes Weep No More

Open Wound

Heal Soon

Sun Rise

Coming Noon

Patched Dirt

Buried Hurt

Lying Beneath

Water Seeps

Seed of Grief

Rest for Now

Now

I Rest

Plant My Soul

The World Of Sin
by
Excel
Inmate #03A5572, Lakeview Shock Incarceration
Correctional Facility, Brocton, New York

I wonder why I was born in a world of sin:

In a world where it seems my life will never begin:

I lay down in my cell sometimes at night and cry cause
    I'm in so much pain:

And if this is a game I don't wanna play:

They say the white man keeps the black man in the joke:

I pray to the white pope but he don't hear me though:

I live in the projects where I smell pissy elevators:

Where I see many black faces, homicide and rape cases:

In a world of sin I will never understand cause I once saw
    the police take a black baby out of a garbage can:

Politicians and legislators are making laws to oppress my
    peoples:

If we are all God's children why can't I be treated equal:

Bill Clinton once said he could feel the pain that we feel:

If that's the case why did he pass the Welfare Reform Bill:

I have come from Africa to America to the ghetto to the
projects to prison and back to the ghetto:

I hear my ancestors were great kings and queens:

But today my reality is penitentiary:

So why was I born in a world of sin:

In a world where it seems my life will never begin.

Long Live The Eager Hearts
by
Comrade George Smith
Inmate #K62548, Centinela State Prison, California

Bear with me:

Why would you try and convince me that the prison
experience is not sickening shit?!

Standing before me pretending to be faithless, an anti-
socialist, even a loyal racist.

Running on and on about wars, scars and battles between
bulls (officers) and convicts.

Glorifying this miserable bullshit!

Now as I sit miserably watching throats and souls slit, I
remember comrade, uncle, friend that you glorified the
"pin."

Making it sound damn good to my siblings and I,
knowing our eager hearts would embrace the thought of
coming to the "pin" simply to get smart and big; instead
of going to school for an intellect, off to the gym for 20-

inch arms and sweat, shit!

Fuck, now I've become a threat ...

A mere child growing old, waging wars against any and all to maintain respect.

Who would have imagined Little George would be next.

Next to be so angry, next to be so pained, watching with an anxious heart to destroy again.

Who would have thought Little George would be so rude, but humbly waiting to hurt everything because nobody told him this part of the game—knowing they could.

After 8 years and 8 months I'm now 26, trippin' that I'm still trapped in this shit.

A cycle of races standing in front of rifles, believing, "It can never be me," until heads and chests are blown, you see?!

Oh, what a harsh awakening waking up next to a grown man, living in a bathroom (basically), listening to lies, sometimes truths, but mainly bullshit depending on the person time and time again.

Imagine this—it's 5:45 a.m. January 10th '05 and most are still asleep.

T.V. has its illusions of prison; everyone doesn't have to wake and go eat.

Feed yourself or die slowly if you choose.

Souljahs who are loyal to their beliefs, leaders, arrogant warriors, blind pawns, cowards, snitches, homosexuals, liars, thiefs, killers, con artists, rapists, and friends all smile upon you as if all is well, but clandestinely they each have ulterior motives that may concern you.

Even the strong crumble, even the honest mumble your secrets, and for freedom they'll each do the shittiest of sins. Fuck Prison!

These are my truths!

Index

235

238   Index